Architectural Shades and Shadows

Architectural Shades and Shadows

Henry McGoodwin

A new edition
with an introduction by
Tony P. Wrenn

The American Institute of Architects Press
Washington, D.C.

The American Institute of Architects Press
1735 New York Avenue, N.W.
Washington, D.C. 20006

First published in 1904 by Bates & Guild Co., Boston. Second impression 1926

Introduction © 1989 by the American Institute of Architects
All rights reserved. Published 1989

Printed in the United States of America
93 92 91 90 89 5 4 3 2 1

Library of Congress Cataloging-in-Publication Data

McGoodwin, Henry. 1871–1927.
Architectural shades and shadows/Henry McGoodwin;
foreword by Tony P. Wrenn.
p.   cm.
Reprint, with new foreword.
Originally published: Boston: Bates & Guild Co., 1926.
ISBN 1-55835-053-5: $32.95.—ISBN 1-55835-059-4 (pbk.): $19.95
1. Shades and shadows.
2. Architectural drawing—Technique.
I. Title.
NA2715.M3 1989
720'.28'4—dc20
89-39971

Designed by Market Sights, Inc.
Type in Century Light by Unicorn Graphics and Kim Vencill
Printed by York Graphic Services, Inc., York, Pennsylvania

Contents

"In casting shadows on
architectural drawings he [the student]
is dealing with materials of art
rather than materials of mathematics."

Henry Kerr McGoodwin's *Architectural Shades and Shadows* was published first in 1904 and reprinted in 1926. It was used for years to teach architects and architectual draftsmen how to give form, depth, and expression to their drawings through the use of shadows. The book covers tools, papers, and techniques and, using a series of drawings and photographs, explains the effect of shadows cast by various architectural elements.

McGoodwin's book belongs to a teaching tradition, but his approach changed both the manner in which the subject was taught and the manner in which it was written about. Before the publication of this book shadow casting had been a subject for mathematicians concerned with geometric formulae. McGoodwin was concerned with the representational power of shades and shadows and dealt with the subject as art rather than mathematics. Never again in American schools of architecture would the subject be purely mechanical. It would be used instead to stress the central importance of drawing to the Beaux-Arts method, to teach the manner in which renderings are given depth and perspective and interest, and to add elegance and subtlety to architectural drawings.

McGoodwin began his teaching career at the University of Pennsylvania in 1901. He was thirty years old and had earned a B.S. degree from Ogden College in Bowling Green, Kentucky, and an S.B. degree in architecture from the Massachusetts Institute of Technology. He earned his Ogden degree in 1891, entered MIT that same year, and graduated in 1894. Returning to Bowling Green, his hometown, he began work as an architect and architectural draftsman. His work took him to Louisville; Charleston, South Carolina; and Columbus, Ohio.[1]

In Philadelphia, as a beginning instructor of architecture in 1901, McGoodwin taught shades and shadows, along with graphics, perspective, rendering, order problems, and design.[2] He had taken shades and shadows ten years earlier at MIT, where it was required in the first term of the second year.[3] At Penn it was required of freshmen and first-year special students in architecture. The 1901 catalog described the three-hour course as "lectures and exercises based on Millard's translation of Pillet's *Shades and Shadows*."[4]

Jules-Jean-Désiré Pillet studied as a consultant at the Ecole des Beaux-Arts in Paris from 1863 to 1868, and began teaching descriptive geometry there in 1874.[5] He was a mathematician/architect who seems to have formalized the shades and shadows curriculum by defining the terms of the course:

> Through the course on Shades and Shadows a distinction in meaning will be observed between the word *Shade* and the word *Shadow*. That portion of a body which is darkened by being turned away from the source of light, and which is bounded by the separatrix [the line between light and dark areas on a partially illuminated surface] will be referred to as the *Shade* of that body; while that portion of a body which is darkened by the interposition of another body, or another part of the same body, between it and the source of light will be referred to as the Shadow of the second body on the first.[6]

Julian Millard, a professor of architecture at the University of Pennsylvania, translated Pillet into English in 1896.[7] On the title page is the subtitle:

> An exposition and demonstration of short and convenient methods for determining the shades and shadows of objects illuminated by the conventional parallel rays: The methods in use at the Ecole des Beaux-Arts at Paris.[8]

Millard noted in his preface that

> The ordinary methods of Descriptive Geometry as commonly applied in Casting Shadows are not well adapted to the hurried conditions of Architectural practice. The result is that Shadows are ordinarily guessed at merely because of insufficient time to work them out by the laborious method. Under such circumstance only those who have studied the subject with great care and much practice can avoid gross and misleading errors. The value of Shadows on Elevations is only beginning to be understood among American draftsmen. Shadows show the projection of the different parts, profiles of moldings, pitch of roofs, reveal of windows and doors, and many other details which could not otherwise be understood without a perspective drawing.[9]

Pillet's work is a work of mathematics, though it includes some examples that are architectural, and it uses the methodology of descriptive geometry. McGoodwin was not a mathematician but an architect, and evidently felt so uncomfortable with Pillet's approach that he began developing his own work. According to McGoodwin, the purpose of his text, published in 1904, was twofold:

> First, to present to the architectural student a course in the casting of architectural shadows, the exposition of which shall be made from the architect's standpoint, in architectural terms, and as clearly and simply as may be; and second, to furnish examples of the shadows of such architectural forms as occur oftenest in practice, which the draftsman may use for reference in drawing shadows when it is impracticable to cast them.

"These do not appear," McGoodwin continued, "to have been the purposes of books on this subject hitherto published, and therefore the preparation of this one seemed justifiable."[10]

To understand the place of this work in architectural teaching and to appreciate his other contributions to architectural education, we must take a quick look at architectural education in America in his era.

When McGoodwin began teaching in 1901, architectural education in America was scarcely older than McGoodwin himself. The nation's oldest school of architecture, established at the Massachusetts Institute of Technology, had held its first classes in September 1868, thirty-three years before. The University of Pennsylvania, the fifth oldest architecture school, where McGoodwin would teach, had been established in 1874 and had reached the ripe old age of twenty-seven. At its founding it joined the University of Illinois (1870), Cornell (1871), and Syracuse (1873), along with MIT. By the end of the century Columbia (1881), Columbian (now George Washington University) (1884), the Armour (now Illinois) Institute of Technology (1889), and Harvard (1895) had also established architecture schools. The University of Michigan began instruction in 1876 but abandoned the curriculum two years later, joining a number of other schools or courses that were planned or operated for only a short time in the nineteenth century.[11]

As the twentieth century began there still were fewer than a dozen schools of architecture in the United States, enrolling only a few hundred students. Most practitioners entered architecture through apprentice training in an established office, and neither they nor their mentors were likely to be overly welcoming to the academically trained architect, especially those trained in such schools as America had to offer. Resources, especially architectural resources, were meager, secondary schools were inadequate, and most architecture departments developed not independently, but within other departments. A few were

SHADES AND SHADOWS

AN EXPOSITION AND DEMONSTRATION OF SHORT AND CONVENIENT METHODS
FOR DETERMINING THE SHADES AND SHADOWS OF OBJECTS
ILLUMINATED BY THE CONVENTIONAL PARALLEL RAYS:
THE METHODS IN USE AT THE ECOLE DES
BEAUX ARTS AT PARIS

FROM THE FRENCH OF

M. JULES PILLET

PROFESSEUR DE GEOMETRIE DESCRIPTIVE A L'ECOLE DES BEAUX ARTS, PROFESSEUR DE PERSPECTIVE
A L'ECOLE DES PONTS ET CHAUSSEES ET A L'ECOLE SPECIALE D'ARCHITECTURE,
MAITRE DE DESSIN DE MACHINES A L'ECOLE POLYTECHNIQUE,
INSPECTEUR DE L'ENSEIGNEMENT DU DESSIN.

TRANSLATED AND REVISED BY

JULIAN MILLARD

ASSISTANT PROFESSOR OF ARCHITECTURE AT THE UNIVERSITY OF PENNSYLVANIA.

PHILADELPHIA:
FRANKLIN PRINTING COMPANY,
514–18 MINOR STREET.
1896.

associated with fine arts schools, but in the main they evolved within engineering departments.

The profession was almost as young as the schools. The American Institute of Architects, formed in New York on February 23, 1857, was not yet fifty years old, and by and large its members had not been academically trained.[12] Only one of the thirteen who attended the first AIA meeting, Richard Morris Hunt (1827–1895), had received a formal architectural education. In 1846 Hunt entered the Ecole des Beaux-Arts in Paris, the first American to study there.[13]

Hunt returned from the Ecole des Beaux-Arts and established his own practice in New York in 1856. The following year he established his atelier. Students of Hunt used his library for exercises—with more than two thousand volumes on architecture alone, it was the largest American library on the subject—and followed the educational method Hunt himself had followed in Paris.[14]

When William Robert Ware (1832–1915), one of Hunt's first students, was asked in 1865 to set up an architecture department at MIT, he agreed, while continuing to teach in the atelier of his own office, Ware and Van Brunt. He evolved a curriculum, put together course materials, and traveled extensively in Europe, studying European architectural schools. Predisposed as he was toward the Ecole, it was natural that Ware instituted courses at MIT that at least embodied the Ecole's spirit.[15]

Increasingly at MIT and elsewhere, the Ecole and its methods came to be the desired course of study. Many students used the MIT and other American courses as a preparatory school for the Ecole, where, in the last decade of the nineteenth century, more than one hundred Americans went to study. As early as 1889 these students had discussed the formation of an Ecole alumni association, finally organized in 1894 as The Society of Beaux-Arts Architects.[16] The society intended to promote the principles of the Ecole and to encourage Americans to attend. They established ateliers, began student competitions, and embarked on an active educational program in association with several of the architectural schools. In a typical program all architectural design instruction was accomplished under the auspices of the society, which issued programs accepted by the schools. All drawings were sent to the society in New York to be judged by Beaux-Arts juries; the judgments and rankings of the society were accepted by the schools. The society even lobbied architects for the creation of an American school of architecture patterned after the Ecole.

Lectures and drawing classes were offered at the Ecole, though the school did little more than control student training in design. The Ecole issued the programs and requirements, assisted students in working out basic schemes, graded final solutions through juries of architects, and exhibited the results. The actual process of guiding the student through design preparation was left to the smaller unit, the atelier. These units were under the supervision of an architect, who provided, for a fee, instruction and a studio in which to work. Usually these ateliers were small, but some included more than a hundred students. The architect/teacher/role model was generally an experienced and well-known architect who, at least in theory, could provide personal attention, advice, and criticism.

The Ecole's students proved its success, and they were, in the nineteenth century and first quarter of the twentieth century, some of the best-known names in American architecture and architectural education. Constant Desire Despradelle (1862–1912), who came to MIT in 1893, and Paul Philippe Cret (1876–1945), who came to the University of Pennsylvania in 1903, had both achieved distinction at the Ecole.[17] Through their students in the United States, and through their own designs, they gained greater distinction. In addition to Richard Morris Hunt, Henry Hobson Richardson, Charles F. McKim, Louis Sullivan, Bernard Maybeck, William Adams Delano, John Wellborn Root II, and Julia Morgan were Ecole students.

One required course they shared in the study of design was shades and shadows, though it was taught more as a technical course than as a design course. The student was expected to be familiar with the elements of geometry and algebra, and the course was normally taught as a part of descriptive geometry. Richard Morris Hunt studied shades and shadows at the Ecole in 1846.[18] Yale offered the subject in inaugurating its School of Engineering in 1852. When John Wiley & Sons of New York published Samuel Edward Warren's *General Problems of Shades and Shadows* in 1867, and again in 1895, Warren noted that

> The study of Shades and Shadows is an application of the general problems of Descriptive Geometry, in connexion with a few physical principles; and of Descriptive Geometry, no one, who has occasion to be conversant with forms, singly or in combination, can know too much, either for practical purposes, or as a promoter, in its peculiar way, of mental power.[19]

Both of Richard Morris Hunt's sons (who would become the Hunt and Hunt firm), Richard Howland Hunt (1862–1931) and Joseph Howland Hunt (1870–1924), took their "shades and shadows" at the Ecole. Joseph Howland Hunt's exercises in shades and shadows while he was a student of Daumet and Esquie (Daumet's assistant) survive, and show typical geometric designs involving cones, squares, circles, a Doric capital, and their shades and shadows. The exercises are labeled "Cours de Mr. Pillet."[20] Indeed, Pillet not only defined the course for the Ecole, but for American schools as well, no matter who wrote the text.

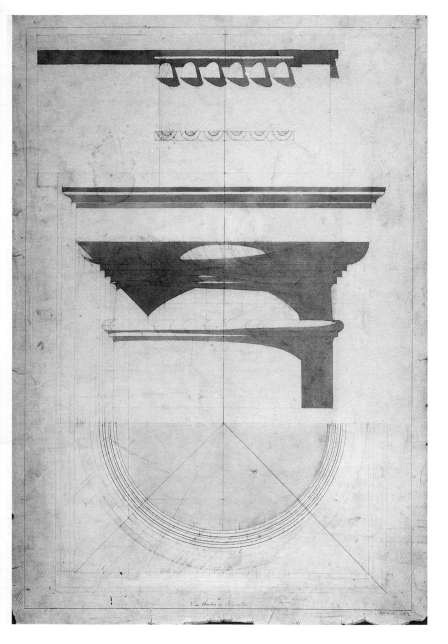

When John Edward Hill, who taught at Cornell, published *A Textbook on Shades and Shadows, and Perspective* in 1894, he gave credit to Pillet. Millard's 1896 translation of Pillet obviously played a major role in teaching the course in American architectural schools. In 1912 William Robert Ware, identified as "formerly Professor of Architecture in the Massachusetts Institute of Technology, Emeritus Professor of Architecture in Columbia University," wrote his own *Shades and Shadows With Applications to Architectural Details and Exercises in Drawing Them With the Brush and Pen,* and acknowledged Pillet.

McGoodwin did not acknowledge Pillet in his 1904 work, although his debt to Pillet is obvious. McGoodwin did not attend the Ecole and probably was never in a Paris atelier.[21] He had, however, studied under Despradelle at MIT, possibly in both his junior and senior years. At Penn he used Pillet as his initial text in teaching shades and shadows and taught with Paul Cret, who came to Penn to teach in 1903. He was therefore no stranger to the Ecole and its methods or to Pillet.

McGoodwin realized that there was a mathematical side to the study of shades and shadows, but he urged the student to view that as "its means—having no greater architectural importance than the scale or triangle or other tools used in making drawings."[22] It disturbed him that the student had

> been asked to study shades and shadows and perspective as parts of descriptive geometry. It is little wonder that his results have often been mistaken and useless, and his study of these subjects spiritless, disinterested and perfunctory.
>
> The student should realize at the outset that in casting shadows on architectural drawings he is dealing with materials of art rather than with materials of mathematics. The shades and shadows of architectural objects are architectural things, not mathematical things. They are architectural entities, having form, mass and proportion just as have other architectural entities. Consequently these masses and shapes of dark must be as carefully considered in the study of design as are columns or entablatures or other masses.[23]

Exercise, Doric capital, from Julian Millard, translator, M. Jules Pillet, Shades and Shadows. (Philadelphia: Franklin Printing Co, 1896). Compare this with Figure 56 in McGoodwin. (AIA Archives)

McGoodwin also sought, within the outline of the shades of shadows course, to use architectural means to educate the student about architectural terms, the components of the orders, and nomenclature. "It is important that [the student] should become thoroughly familiar with the orders and other elements of architectural compositions," he wrote, and "equally important that he should become quite as familiar with the shadows of these elements."[24] McGoodwin's work is filled with drawings of specific orders, from specific sources, and, in his discussion of the shadows of each, the architectural terminology is quite specific: "the shadow of the fillet on the abacus"; "the shadow of the ovolo on the neck of the column"; "shadows on the raking mouldings of the pediment"; "shadows of those mouldings on the tympanum." Other works on the subject had used architectural illustrations, but not as many as McGoodwin and never before as fully described.

McGoodwin introduced one additional element to his study: photography. Using models, he set up examples of the shades and shadows in his exercises. With the proper lighting, the shadows of freestanding and engaged columns and capitals of the various orders are shown. It is one thing to show the shadows in a drawing, quite another to prove one's assertions through the use of photographs. McGoodwin set the stage for this approach by beginning his book with three representations, from the offices of Hunt and Hunt, of the facade of the Metropolitan Museum in New York: a line drawing in which shade and shadows play no part, a rendering of the same facade in which shade and shadows give the building perspective, and a photograph of the building from the same angle and with the same light, proving the accuracy of the detail and depth of the rendering.[25]

It is with shadows that the designer models his building, gives it texture, "color," relief, proportions. Imagine a building executed in pure white marble and exposed, not to sunlight, but to uniformly diffused light that would cast no shadows. The building would have no other apparent form than that of its contour. It would seem as flat as a great unbroken wall. Cornices, colonnades, all details, all projections within the contour lines would disappear. The beauty of all the carefully wrought details, the fine balance and proportion of masses that had engaged the skill and enthusiasm of the designer, would vanish.[26]

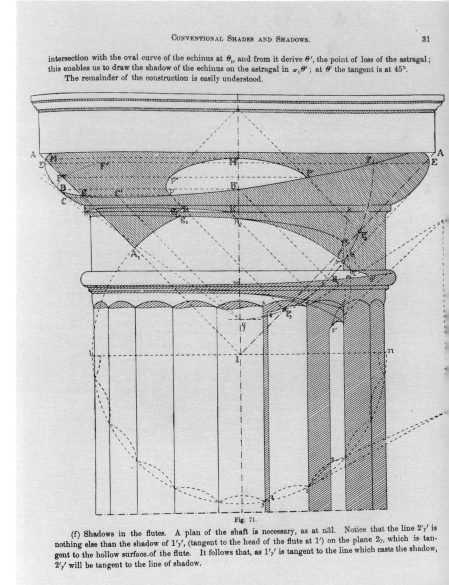

intersection with the oval curve of the echinus at $\theta_{,,}$ and from it derive θ', the point of loss of the astragal; this enables us to draw the shadow of the echinus on the astragal in σ, θ'; at θ' the tangent is at 45°. The remainder of the construction is easily understood.

Fig. 71.

(f) Shadows in the flutes. A plan of the shaft is necessary, as at n31. Notice that the line $2'\gamma'$ is nothing else than the shadow of $1'\gamma'$, (tangent to the head of the flute at $1'$) on the plane 2_{γ}, which is tangent to the hollow surface of the flute. It follows that, as $1'\gamma'$ is tangent to the line which casts the shadow, $2'\gamma'$ will be tangent to the line of shadow.

One could not draw well without understanding and interpreting shades and shadows, he insisted, noting that "it is as impossible to separate the expression of the architect's idea from the technique of his drawings as to separate the technique of a musician from the expression of the composer's idea."[27] Not averse to a bit of hyperbole, McGoodwin insisted that "indeed—leaving out of account considerations of construction and of the practical requirements of planning—no purely aesthetic consideration so greatly influences design as does that of shadows."[28]

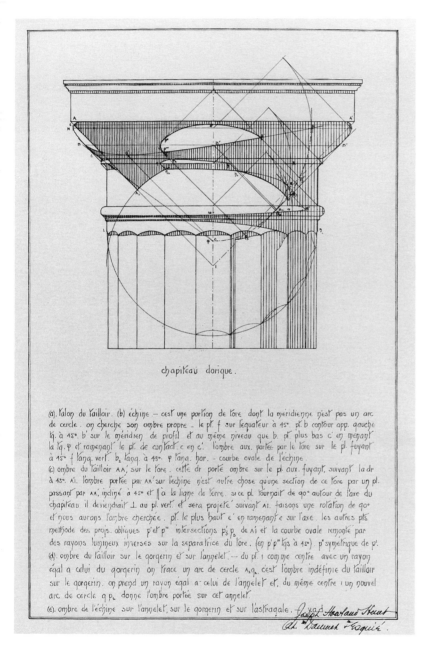

McGoodwin dedicated his book to Professor Frances W. Chandler (1844–1925) of MIT, "whose kindly influence has long been an aid and an inspiration to hundreds of those young architects who are engaged in the effort to fitly establish their art in America, and to excel in it."[29] Chandler was head of the department at MIT when McGoodwin entered. He had been a student of Ware and Van Brunt in their atelier, and had studied at the Daumet atelier in Paris, where he shared rooms with and traveled with Robert S. Peabody and Charles Follen McKim. Through both his teaching and his writings, he had a profound influence on his students during the twenty-three years that he headed the department at MIT.

McGoodwin also credited two of his classmates in the class of 1894 at MIT. Harry Wentworth Gardner (1873–1954),[30] one of these, joined the faculty at MIT in 1895, a year after his graduation, and taught for forty-eight years, not retiring until 1943. Gardner, whose "criticism and advice has been most helpful"[31] according to McGoodwin, wrote his own *Shades and Shadows* for the American School of Correspondence at the Armour Institute of Technology in Chicago. Issued first as an instructional paper in 1903, the work was published as part of Armour's *Cyclopedia of Drawing* in 1905.[32]

Frederick Maynard Mann (1868–?),[33] the other McGoodwin classmate, was at Washington University in St. Louis in 1904.[33] He gave "assistance in the preparation of the book"[34] according to McGoodwin. Mann taught at Penn, Washington University, and the University of Illinois before going, in 1913, to the University of Minnesota, where he founded the architecture department.

Frederick Law Olmsted, Jr. (1870–1957),[35] who graduated from Harvard in 1894, may have known McGoodwin, Mann, and Gardner while they were at MIT. They certainly would have known that Olmsted, a well-known photographer, had been the photographer for the McMillan Park Commission plan for Washington. It may well be for that reason that his "lens" was used in making the photographs. The actual photographs were shot at "half-past eight o'clock in the morning, in Philadelphia, in the latter part of August."[36] T. B. Temple of Philadelphia assisted in the preparation of the photographs, and models were provided by Charles Emmel, whose company provided "architectural moldings for exterior and interior uses and fine carvings and artificial marble."[37] It is possible that some of Emmel's details had been used in classes at MIT, and it is obvious that Olmsted and McGoodwin knew him and his

Joseph Howland Hunt, Ecole des Beaux-Arts, "The Three General Methods for Finding Shadows," exercise from "Cours de Mr. Pillet," 1895. (Prints and Drawings Collection, Octagon Museum, American Architectural Foundation)

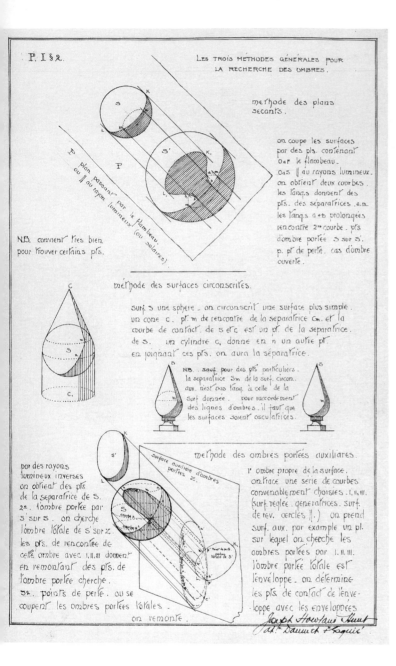

work. Emmel's company was profitable enough by 1898 to have a division in Chicago as well as the one in Boston. McGoodwin chose Emmel's "Scamozzi Capitals," "Corinthian Capitals," "Angular Ionic Capitals," and "Erechtheum Capitals."[38] Naturally, McGoodwin used a Boston-based publisher, Bates and Guild.

Whatever the assistance given by others, the text is undeniably the work of McGoodwin, and the particularly fine drawings are by his hand.

It is not clear why McGoodwin gravitated toward architecture. He may have known or been influenced by Bowling Green architects Creedmore Fleenor (1860–1925) or architect-builder Thomas Milburn, whose son Frank Pierce Milburn (1868–1926) would have been a contemporary of McGoodwin in Bowling Green.[39] McGoodwin seems to have been very good at drawing even though a hunting accident sometime between his thirteeth and eighteenth year almost ended the possibility of studying architecture. McGoodwin was not ambidexterous at the time of the accident; he drew with his right hand. The loss of his drawing hand was total, between the wrist and the elbow, and he later wore a prosthesis and glove. McGoodwin had to learn to write and, more important, to draw, all over again, with his left hand.[40] The plates in this work prove he learned well. The source of his inspiration to relearn is not known, but he certainly had one of the finest teachers in the world in Despradelle at MIT.[41] McGoodwin would later write about his years at MIT that

> My most painful memory of the Institute is useless lectures in Physics, Light and Heat. I believe that in the architectural department, courses in Physics, Chemistry, Light and Heat, Electricity, etc., should be made optional for students who do not take options in construction, that architectural students should be taught all courses in sciences, under instructors in architecture as far as possible, that the department should be housed in a building of architectural worth.[42]

McGoodwin returned to Bowling Green after his 1894 graduation and secured work. His report to MIT does not indicate for whom he worked, but between 1894 and 1896 he worked as a draftsman in Bowling Green. In 1896 he moved to Louisville, where he worked as a draftsman with the firm of H. P. McDonald. At some point in 1897, he transferred to the Snead Iron Works Co., also as a draftsman, remaining there until 1898. He returned to Bowling Green in 1899 as an architectural draftsman with the Bowling Green Stone Company but left that same year for Charleston, South Carolina, where he practiced

Draw rays tangent to each of these curves at a and b on the first curve, and at m and n on the second; these are points of the separatrix.

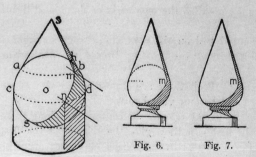

Fig. 3.

The first tangents, through a and b, if prolonged, intersect the second curve in a_1 and b_1 and are points of the shadow of the first surface on the second.

Repeat the operation by making as many slices as are necessary and join points of the same kind by continuous curves; we then obtain in KabL and in mppn the two separatrices and in $K_1a_1ppb_1L_1$ the shadow cast by S on S'.

The points p and p, where the shadow is lost in the shade, are called "points of loss." They do not always exist. (See Fig. 4.) In the case of Figure 4 the shadow is called "*closed*," and in Figure 3 it is called "*open*."

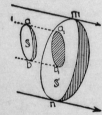

Fig. 4.

This method is in general one of difficult application. It is very convenient, however, in finding particular points of the line of shadow.

SECOND. *Method of circumscribing surfaces.*—Assume a surface (a sphere for example) of which the separatrix is to be determined. (Fig. 5.) Circumscribe about it a more simple surface, a cone for example, the separatrix of which is supposed to be known (a straight line in the case of a cone). The point m, where this straight line intersects the curve of contact ab of the cone and the surface, is a point of the separatrix of the latter (evident).

We may take a cylinder tangent to the sphere along the curve cd, which gives in n another point of the separatrix. Joining hmn and g by a continuous curve we have the required separatrix.

NOTE.—Except for certain particular cases, the separatrix Sm of the auxiliary circumscribing surface is not tangent to the line hmng of the given surface. In other words, when two surfaces are tangent their lines of shade are not always tangent. The lines of shade are tangent only when the contact of the two surfaces is what is called osculatory. (The contact of two lines is osculatory when, at the point of contact, the radius of curvature of the two lines is the same.)

The contact will be osculatory if the profile is drawn free-hand (Fig. 7), as is generally done in architecture.

THIRD. *Method of auxiliary shadows or method of oblique projections.*—Assume two surfaces, S and S' (Fig. 8), upon which it is desired to perform all the operations in shades and shadows indicated below.

Fig. 5.   Fig. 6.   Fig. 7.

(a) *Shade*[1] *on the surface S.*

1st. On the surface S draw a series of curves, No. 1, No. 2, No. 3, conveniently chosen.

In choosing these sections two things are essential:

(a) The lines of section should be of simple form, so as to be easily cast on the Auxiliary Plane;
(b) they should all be of the same form.

2d. Take arbitrarily an auxiliary surface Z, ordinarily a plane, upon which are found in No. 1', No. 2', No. 3', the shadows of the above curves.

---

[1] Throughout the course on Shades and Shadows a distinction in meaning will be observed between the word *shade* and the word *shadow.*

That portion of a body which is darkened by being turned away from the source of light, and which is bounded by the separatrix, will be referred to as the *shade* of that body; while that portion of a body which is darkened by the interposition of another body, or another part of the same body, between it and the source of light will be referred to as the *shadow* of the second body on the first.

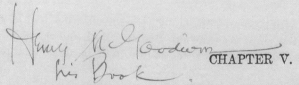

CHAPTER V.

SHADOWS OF CONVEX CYLINDERS.

§ 19. SHADOW OF AN ABACUS. (Fig. 48.)

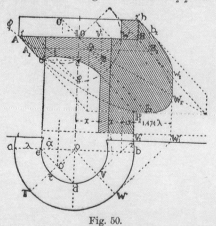

The abacus has a projection λ beyond the shaft of the column at front and sides. The axis of the column stands in front of the wall at a distance α, ordinarily equal to $\frac{1}{3}$ R (R being the radius of the shaft).

The shadow on the shaft is, according to Chapter III, a circle described about O_1 as a centre. This circle is only used between A_1, shadow of the left angle A of the abacus, and P, the point of loss.

The vertical line through P is the shade on the shaft; N_2 is a point of the shadow on the wall and its distance from the shade line is $x + \alpha$.

Fig. 48.

The rest of the drawing is easily comprehended; note that no plan is needed; the knowledge of the distance α is sufficient.

§ 20. APPLICATION.

Doric guttæ and their fillet. (Fig. 49.) The profile at the left enables us to find in a_1c_1 the shadow of the architrave fillet on the fillet of the guttæ and in a_2c_2 the shadow of the latter on the architrave (interrupted by the guttæ).

Fig. 49.

Suppose that the guttæ are cylinders whose axes are at distance α from the wall. The fillet md_1 casts shadow on the guttæ in arcs of circles having O_1 and O as centres. The points of loss, p,p, correspond to the points of change, p_2,p_2, on the architrave. Finally, the circles at the base of the guttæ cast half ellipses inscribed in the half parallelograms $J_1f_1f_1$. The figure shows the construction.

§ 21. SHADOW OF A CIRCULAR CAP ON A COLUMN. (Fig. 50.)

Axis of column $\frac{1}{3}$ R in front of wall.

(a) Shadow cast on the shaft.

FIRST. Find in W and V the shades on the two cylinders.

SECOND. Point of loss. A circle of radius OW is the shadow of AB on the 45° oblique plane. The point where this arc crosses VS, since it lies in the surface of the cylinder and also in the line of the

Fig. 50.

architecture in late 1899 and early 1900. In 1900 he went to Cleveland to work as a draftsman with F. I. Packard. In 1901 he was offered the position of instructor in architecture at the University of Pennsylvania, a position he held until 1904.[43]

The Department of Architecture at Pennsylvania had some 55 students in 1901 when McGoodwin taught his first classes. The number grew to 65 the next year, to 85 in 1903, and to 106 during the school year 1903–04.[44] McGoodwin, in addition to his own classes, taught "Elements of Architecture" with Melvin Powers Laird in 1902–03 and added "Design," which he also shared with Laird, in 1903–04.

McGoodwin moved to Washington University in St. Louis, whose school of architecture had been founded in 1902, to teach for the years 1905 and 1906. His "A Plea" for a More Liberal System of Education in Architecture" was published by the university in the spring of 1906. In discussing architectural training, McGoodwin wrote

> That training affects, directly and indirectly, the comfort and convenience, the physical and moral health of the whole people; for it affects our efficiency in organizing the mass of humanly wrought material with which civilized life must surround itself. Stated broadly, the business of the architect is to put men's surroundings in order; to seek and to establish just relations among the objects of men's creation, to introduce harmony or arrangement among them. More specially it is to "design" the most convenient, wholesome and beautiful streets, parks, play-grounds, homes, hospitals, offices, factories, churches; to save light and air and material; and to avoid all waste of effort, of energy, of resources, by his skill in these designs. In short, it is the architect's business to make the best possible surroundings for human work, play, rest, and worship, surroundings best designed to satisfy sense and sensibilities and to save money, labor, time and health. ... The disorder which results to a community by reason of an inefficient police force is a bagatelle compared to that which results by reason of an inefficient architectural profession.[45]

McGoodwin called for an intern program to be brought about by a change in methods, "to allow and encourage, or even require, students to engage in practice in architects' offices."[46] He advocated a system in which the teaching of design would be accomplished either in the drafting rooms at the school or in a number of accredited ateliers conducted by practicing architects.

> Even, if some students preferred to take their academic training, as now, in a comparatively short period devoted entirely to study, the influence on these of a body of mature men who preferred to combine practice with schooling and to remain in connection with a school for six or eight or a dozen years, would be invaluable; an influence similar to that of the *ancien [sic]* in the *ateliers* of Paris . . . .[47]

He supported a system of central and atelier training and noted, "such a system has been in operation at the Ecole des Beaux-Arts for upward of three-quarters of a century; and it may be asserted without any fear of exaggeration that the graduates of this institution have produced the only body of consistent and vital architectural work executed during that time."[48]

McGoodwin undoubtedly used the *Architectural Shades and Shadows* text in his courses at Washington University, and it remained in use there after he left.[49]

By 1907–08 McGoodwin had moved to Carnegie Technical Schools in Pittsburgh, where the catalog listed him as an instructor in architectural practice in the School of Applied Design.[50] By 1909, the year he joined the American Institute of Architects, he had become an associate professor of architecture and acting dean of the School of Applied Design. "The determination of Shades and Shadows as they occur on architectural rendered drawings" was a required course. By 1910–11 McGoodwin had become one of the officers of administration of the school, and was still acting dean of the twenty-four-person faculty. By 1912–13, with changes in the makeup of the department, McGoodwin was a professor of architecture and in charge of the Department of Architecture.

In 1914, after a visit to the School of Architecture at Carnegie, C. C. Zantzinger of the AIA Committee on Education described the School of Architecture in terms that reveal the influence of McGoodwin's ideas:

> The School of Architecture has established a certain fixed quantity of work which each student must do to become eligible for a degree. This can be accomplished generally in four years. The length of time spent in the accomplishment of the required work however, has no bearing on the degree. Under this system a student may accomplish his college course while actively working in an office.

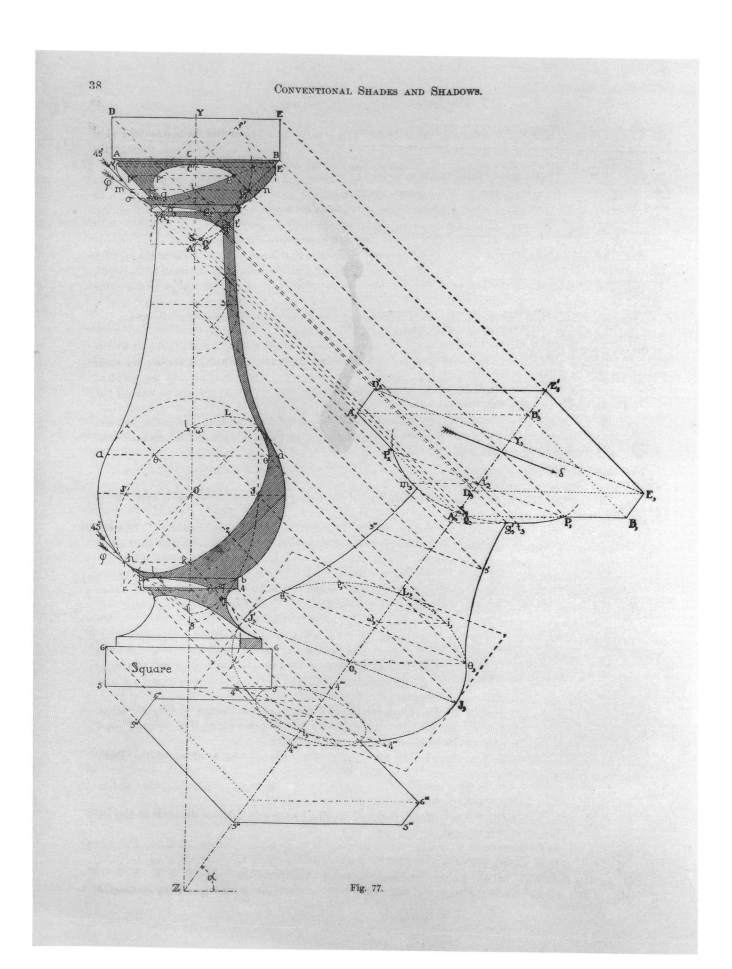

Fig. 77.

"Shadows of a Baluster," from problem given at the Ecole des Beaux-Arts by Pillet, March 6, 1886. Compare this with the following illustration. (AIA Archives)

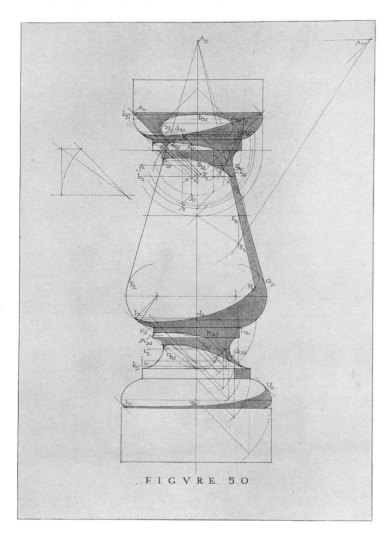

FIGVRE 50

In the matter of making judgments the school had adopted the jury system for the free hand and life drawing, water color and modelling. The professors of the allied schools participate in the judgments and consequently the professor's personal knowledge of a possible prejudice for his pupil, can have no unfair influence.

All architectural design is done under the auspices of the Society of Beaux-Arts Architects of New York. Their programmes as issued, are accepted as the school's, and all drawings are sent to New York for judgment, the ranking of the drawings by the Society's jury being accepted as final by the school.[51]

McGoodwin left Carnegie in July 1918, after being engaged as an architect by the U.S. Steel Corporation in connection with a housing project for Neville Island Arsenal.[52]

In 1919 he was nominated for fellowship in the American Institute of Architects and elected. That year he also moved back to Philadelphia and resumed private practice, living in Lumberville and maintaining offices in Philadelphia. He returned to Carnegie in 1923 as dean and chairman of the faculty of the College of Fine Arts, known previously as the School of Applied Design. He held that position until 1925–26.[53]

In 1912 McGoodwin had been one of the eight founders of the Association of Collegiate Schools of Architecture, formed in Washington during the forty-sixth convention of the AIA. The purpose of the ACSA was to "promote the efficiency of architectural education," and Carnegie Institute of Technology was one of the charter members.[54] In 1913 he suggested that the AIA and its chapters establish a relationship with students through awards and medals, and his proposal led to the establishment of the AIA School Medal.[55]

Already ill when he returned to Carnegie in 1923, McGoodwin was forced to retire and return to Lumberville in 1925. "His illness was one that baffled physicians and nerve specialists, and it was only his indomitable spirit and will power which carried him through four years of suffering." He died on January 30, 1927.[56]

The president and the executive board of the Carnegie Institute of Technology adopted a resolution on his death, noting that

The Department of Architecture is entirely his creation, firmly established by his exquisite taste and lofty standards. And from the early days of the College of Fine Arts, his strict ideals and wise foresight deeply affected the policies of the whole college, and during his too brief term, when he was its Head, brought it to its highest point of prosperity and well being.[57]

A resolution inscribed by the ACSA at McGoodwin's death in 1927 called his work at Carnegie "his culminating achievement" and continued:

He left the imprint of his character upon the minds of many young men.

His intellect, his clarity of vision, his powers of leadership, his courage, honesty and sense of humor are well remembered by his students and Fellow teachers.

As one of the founders and guiding spirits of this association, his loss is keenly felt by its members.[58]

Shades and shadows continued to be taught until after World War II. It is still taught in many places, though seldom as a separate course. As late as 1950 in a survey of architects, Graphics/Shades and Shadows was ranked number ten in importance of all courses offered in architecture schools. When teachers of architecture who were also licensed architects were asked to rank the same courses—some twenty-six courses were included in the rankings—Graphics/Shades and Shadows moved up to seventh place.[59]

McGoodwin's advice to young architects might well be taken by all architects, whatever their age. The architect should, he insisted, look at buildings.

> It will be of great interest and benefit to the student to observe carefully actual shadows on executed work. This observation will familiarize him with the shadows of common architectural forms, and with those of forms less common, as well, which it would be difficult to cast with certainty unless he had a generally correct intuition of the form such shadows should take. It will increase his power of visualization—of seeing mentally how and why the shadows of an object take certain forms. It will also help him give his rendering of shadows on drawings the greatest possible interpretative *[sic]* force. Above all, it will train him to a just perception of the effects of actual shadows and of their relation to design; will suggest to him how to obtain those shadows that will give the effects and the proportions he desires, and how to avoid unpleasing shadow effects; and it will awaken in him, as no studies on paper can do, the perception and enjoyment of the play of light and shadow over a facade or any well-modeled object—with its subtle gradations of tone, and sharp notes of accent and contrast. When the student has learned to see and to enjoy these effects, his work in design will take on a new spirit and vitality. For all hope of good artistic work must begin with the joy in it and in the effort to produce it.[60]

Tony P. Wrenn, Archivist
American Institute of Architects

1. Massachusetts Institute of Technology, *Decennial Catalogue*, June 1904, Class of 1894, pp. 68–69. Copies of at least two manuscript biographies of unknown origin exist in Record Group 804, SR 5, AIA Archives. McGoodwin also is included in most of the standard biographical sources.

2. University of Pennsylvania, Catalog, 1901–1902, p. 169.

3. Massachusetts Institute of Technology, Catalog, 1891–1892, p. 37.

4. University of Pennsylvania, Catalog, 1901–1902, p. 109.

5. *Dictionnaire national des contemporains*, tôme 5 (Paris, n.d.), pp. 79–80.

6. M. Jules Pillet, *Shades and Shadows*, translated and revised by Julian Millard (Philadelphia: Franklin Printing Co., 1896), p. 6. This text is in a footnote and it is not certain whether it is Pillet or Millard. It is so basic to the course, however, that one assumes it is Pillet.

7. Ibid.

8. Ibid., title page.

9. Ibid., preface.

10. Henry McGoodwin, *Architectural Shades and Shadows* (Boston: Bates & Guild Co., 1904), p. 1. Page numbers used here refer to the 1904 edition of the work, not to this one. The volume was republished once before, in 1926, by the same publisher.

11. Turpin Bannister, *The Architect at Mid-Century* (New York: Reinhold, 1954), pp. 97–98.

12. RG 509, SR 2, *Minutes*, February 23, 1857, AIA Archives.

13. See Richard Chafee, "Hunt in Paris," in Susan R. Stein, editor, *The Architecture of Richard Morris Hunt* (Chicago: The University of Chicago Press, 1986), pp. 13–46.

14. See William A. Coles, "Richard Morris Hunt and His Library as Revealed in the Studio Sketchbooks of Henry Van Brunt," *Art Quarterly* 30 (Fall/Winter 1967): 224–38.

15. William A. Coles, "William R. Ware" and "Ware and Van Brunt," Adolf K. Placzek, editor, *Macmillan Encyclopedia of Architects* (New York: The Free Press, 1982), vol. 4, pp. 373–76.

16. Bannister, p. 99.

17. "Master Draftsmen, XI: Désiré Despradelle, 1862–1912," *Pencil Points*, May 1925, pp. 59–70, RG 504, AIA *Proceedings*, Convention, 1903, "Report of the Committee on Education," H. L. Warren, Chair, p. 88, AIA Archives.

18. Drawings survive in the Prints and Drawings Collection, Octagon Museum, American Architectural Foundation.

19. Samuel Edward Warren, *General Problems of Shades and Shadows* (New York: John Wiley & Sons, 1867), preface.

20. Two notebooks of shades and shadows exercises survive in the Prints and Drawings Collection, Octagon Museum, American Architectural Foundation.

21. See Henry F. Withey and Elsie Rathburn Withey, *Biographical Dictionary of American Architects Deceased* (Los Angeles: New Age, 1956), pp. 406–7, and C. Julian Oberwarth and William B. Scott, Jr., *A History of the Profession of Architecture in Kentucky* (Louisville: Kentucky State Board of Examiners and Registration of Architects, 1987), p. 2. Although both sources state that McGoodwin attended the Ecole, the Ecole's own records indicate that he did not attend. Moreover, his schedule in Paris would have left no time for study in an atelier.

22. Ibid.

23. (McGoodwin), p. 11.

24. Ibid.

25. Ibid., Figure 1.

26. Ibid., p. 12.

27. Ibid., p. 11.

28. Ibid., p. 12.

29. See "Architects Honor Professor Chandler," *Technology Review* 13 (November 1911): 532–533; and RG 804, SR 5 By Name, AIA Archives.

30. See "Professor Harry Wentworth Gardner," Alumni Supplement, *Technique*, 1936, and RG 804, SR 5, By Name, AIA Archives.

31. McGoodwin, p. 7

32. *Cyclopedia of Drawing*. Also includes papers on "Mechanical Drawing," "Perspective Drawing," "Freehand Drawing," "Pen & Ink Rendering," "Rendering in Wash," and "Architectural Lettering."

33. RG 804, SR 5, By Name, AIA Archives.

34. McGoodwin, p. 7.

35. See *Dictionary of American Biography*, 6th Supplement, pp. 485–486, and RG 804, SR 5, By Name, AIA Archives.

36. McGoodwin, p. 96.

37. Two Charles Emmel catalogs survive in the Library of Congress Collections: *Specimens of Relief Ornamentation for Interior and Exterior Decoration* (Boston, 1895) and *Architectural Modelings for Exterior and Interior Uses* (Chicago, The H. O. Shepard Co., 1898). The Chicago catalog contains the models used by McGoodwin; the quotation is from its title page.

38. Ibid.

39. McGoodwin's father, Isaac Daniel McGoodwin, was a merchant. Henry Kerr was one of five children, the youngest of whom, Robert McGoodwin, was a distinguished architect and teacher at the University of Pennsylvania. Fifteen years Henry's junior, Robert was brought to Philadelphia by Henry to finish high school and study at the University of Pennsylvania. Robert's son Daniel, also an architect, has been most helpful in supplying material to this writer in a number of telephone interviews.

40. Information supplied to the author by McGoodwin's nephew, Daniel McGoodwin, July 5, 1989.

41. Despradelle was included in *Pencil Points*' "Master Draftsmen" (May 1925) series in the 1920s, along with such other masters as Henry Bacon and Otto Eggers.

42. *Decennial Catalogue*, MIT, Class of 1894, p. 69.

43. Ibid.

44. RG 504, AIA, *Proceedings*, Convention, 1904, "Report of the Committee on Education," H. L. Warren, Chair, p. 60.

45. Henry Kerr McGoodwin, "A Plea for a More Liberal System of Education in Architecture," *The Bulletin of the Washington University Association* (April 1906): 35–36.

46. Ibid., p. 40.

47. Ibid., p. 44.

48. Ibid.

49. Letter, March 14, 1977, Dorothy A. Brockhoff, Washington University, to Allison McRavish, AIA Foundation, indicates that Professor Buford Pickens used the McGoodwin work in his classes at Washington University for many years.

50. Carnegie Technical Schools, Catalog, 1906, School of Applied Design, p. 208. All information on McGoodwin's years and titles at Carnegie came from the catalogs for the appropriate years. Of these the Library of Congress has a remarkable collection, as it does of the catalogs of other schools where McGoodwin studied or taught.

51. RG 504, AIA, *Proceedings*, Convention, 1914, "Report of the Committee on Education," C. C. Zantzinger, Chair, pp. 76–77.

52. RG 504, AIA, *Proceedings*, Convention 1919, p. 58. In McGoodwin's nomination to fellowship in the AIA.

53. *The Technology Review*, 29 [1926–1927] (July 1927): 501. Illness seems to have prohibited him for completing the final term.

54. Association of Collegiate Schools of Architecture, Minutes, vol. 5, 1942–1944 (following attendance list for Annual Meeting), "Articles of Organization of Association of Collegiate Schools of Architecture."

55. RG 504, AIA, *Proceedings*, Convention, 1913, "Report of the Committee on Exducation," C. C. Zantzinger, Chair, p. 30; ibid., 1914, pp. 79–80.

56. *The Technology Review* 29 [1926–1927] (July 1927): 501.

57. Ibid.

58. RG 804, SR 5, Henry Kerr McGoodwin, AIA Archives.

59. Bannister, pp. 140–142.

60. McGoodwin, p. 15.

A Note on the 1989 Edition

The original drawings for *Architectural Shades and Shadows*, used in the production of the new edition of this work, are part of the holdings of the Prints and Drawings Collection, Octagon Museum, American Architectural Foundation. The first edition of this work is a part of the Rare Books Collection of the American Institute of Architects Library. The copy of Julian Millard's translation of Jules Pillet's *Shades and Shadows*, used by McGoodwin in his classes at the University of Pennsylvania before the 1904 publication of his own book, is in the AIA Archives. The copy of McGoodwin's book was a gift to the AIA of Henry H. Saylor, and the drawings and the copy of the Pillet work were gifts of Robert McGoodwin. Materials in all three collections are open to the public for research and reference.

A great many people assisted in the research and other work on this project. Among them were Sherry Birk, curator, Prints and Drawings Collection, Octagon Museum, American Architectural Foundation, who first suggested the republication of the McGoodwin work; Leslie O'Brien, AIA Library; Martin Aurand, architectural archivist, University Libraries, and Judith C. Kampert, assistant head, College of Fine Arts, Department of Architecture, both at Carnegie Mellon; Sally Beddow and Kathy Marquis, both at MIT Museum, Massachusetts Institute of Technology; Roger G. Reed, Maine Historic Commission; and Morrison Heckscher, Metropolitan Museum of Art. Other individuals who were particularly helpful were Richard Chafee, Melissa Houghton, Daniel McGoodwin, George E. Pettengill, Millie Riley, George E. Thomas, and John Wells. Lee Stallsworth, photographer, was responsible for all copy work for the volume. The AIA Press provided editorial and production supervision. Marilyn Worseldine updated the graphics and layout of the original work.

T.P.W.

ARCHITECTURAL
SHADES AND SHADOWS

BY HENRY McGOODWIN

INSTRUCTOR IN ARCHITECTURE AT THE
UNIVERSITY OF PENNSYLVANIA

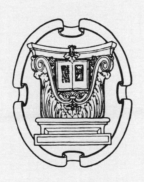

BOSTON

BATES & GUILD COMPANY

1904

To Professor Francis W. Chandler, of the Massachusetts Institute of Technology, whose kindly influence has long been an aid and an inspiration to hundreds of those young architects who are engaged in the effort to fitly establish their art in America, and to excel in it, this book is respectfully inscribed.

H. McG.

Preface

The purpose of this book is twofold: first, to present to the architectural student a course in the casting of architectural shadows, the exposition of which shall be made from the architect's standpoint, in architectural terms, and as clearly and simply as may be; and second, to furnish examples of the shadows of such architectural forms as occur oftenest in practice, which the draftsman may use for reference in drawing shadows when it is impracticable to cast them.

These do not appear to have been the purposes of books on this subject hitherto published, and therefore the preparation of this one has seemed justifiable.

In the discussions of problems no greater knowledge of geometry has been assumed on the part of the student than is in the possession of most architectural draftsmen of a little experience. Consequently the text accompanying some of the problems is longer and more elementary than would otherwise have been necessary.

The author desires to acknowledge here the assistance, in the preparation of the book, of Prof. F.M. Mann, of Washington University, and of Prof. H.W. Gardner, of the Massachusetts Institute of Technology, whose criticism and advice have been most helpful; of Mr. Charles Emmel, of Boston, who furnished the models of which photographs are published hereafter; of Mr. T.B. Temple, of Philadelphia, who assisted in the preparation of these photographs; of Mr. F.L. Olmsted, whose lens was used in making them; of Mr. Hunt, who furnished for reproduction the drawings of the Metropolitan Museum of Art; of the Department of Architecture of the Institute of Technology which furnished for reproduction the drawing by Mr. Stevens; and, finally, of the publishers, to whose interest and painstaking care will be due much of whatever success the work may have.

The Point of View

The student should realize at the outset that in casting shadows on architectural drawings he is dealing with materials of art rather than with materials of mathematics. The shades and shadows of architectural objects are architectural things, not mathematical things. They are architectural entities, having form, mass and proportion just as have other architectural entities. Consequently these masses and shapes of dark must be as carefully considered in the study of design as are columns or entablatures, or other masses. It is, therefore, of great importance to the draftsman or designer that he should be familiar with the forms of those shadows which are most common in architectural work, and with the methods most convenient for determining these and shadows in general.

The student is urged, then, to regard the mathematical part of the study of architectural shadows not as its object or its essence, but merely as its means—having no greater architectural importance than the scale or triangle or other tools used in making drawings. Therefore the use of mathematical terminology has been, as far as possible, avoided in the following discussions.

It has also been thought best to avoid presenting more than one method of solving any given problem, the purpose being to give that one which appears most likely to be convenient in practice and comprehensible to the student.

It has been common in the schools to teach the orders carefully as to form and proportion, with no mention of the shadows which invariably accompany those orders and modify their proportions wherever they are lighted by the sun. The student has been encouraged to spend weeks or perhaps months in learning to draw the architectural elements with great precision, yet without consideration of those masses and shapes of dark which have largely influenced the development and must always influence the use of these elements. Now, if it is of importance that he should become thoroughly familiar with the order and other elements of architectural compositions, it is equally important that he should become quite as familiar with the shadows of those elements. If, moreover, it is important that he should be able to draw the orders and other elements readily, accurately, and with a sure, precise, artistically expressive "touch" or technique, is it not quite as important that he should draw their shadows with an equal ease, precision and expressiveness?

This last, it may be objected, is an affair of drawing and rendering, not involved in the knowledge of the principles of casting shadows. But, as before suggested, these "principles" have no final value in architectural work, and are useful only as means to expression. It is impossible, therefore, to separate the right study of elements of architecture from the expression, that is, the drawing and rendering of them. All architectural drawings—if they be really architectural—will have for their purpose and result the expression of an artistic conception. It is as impossible to separate the expression of the architect's idea from the technique of his drawings as to separate the technique of a musician from the expression of the composer's idea.

These things have not been clearly and generally put to the student of architectural shades and shadows, if they have been put at all. He has been asked to study shades and shadows and perspective as parts of descriptive geometry. It is little wonder that his results have often been mistaken and useless, and his study of these subjects spiritless, disinterested and perfunctory. He is usually keenly alive to and interested in whatever vitally concerns his art, and if once convinced that the subject of shadows does so concern his art, he will bring to the study of it an interest and enthusiasm that will produce results of artistic value.

The Practical Importance
of the Study of Shadows

As suggested in the preceding article the practical importance of the study of architectural shades and shadows lies in two points: in the rendering of drawings— the expression of the artist's idea; and in the study of design—the perfecting of the artist's idea.

As to the first point it may be said that in office practice it is always the most important drawings that are rendered, and it is imperative, therefore, that the shadows on them be drawn and rendered as well as knowledge, skill, and care may make possible. Nothing can add more to the beauty and expressiveness of a drawing than well-drawn and well-rendered shadows; and, contrary to the general belief of inexperienced draftsmen, the value of shadows in adding to the expressiveness of a drawing depends far more on the drawing of those shadows than on the rendering of them. If the shadows are drawn with precision and a good technique, the drawing will look "rendered" to a surprising degree even before any washes have been laid; and the very lightest washes, with a few strong, carefully placed spots to give accent and interest, will make a very effective as well as a very quickly executed rendering; one that will give a far better effect than one in which the shadows are hastily and badly drawn to save time, which is then lavishly expended on a laborious system of washes.

But before and far above this consideration of draftsmanship and rendering in the expression of the artist's idea lies the consideration of the importance of shadows in the study of design—in the *attainment* of the idea and the perfecting of it.

It is with shadows that the designer models his building, gives it texture, "color," relief, proportions. Imagine a building executed in pure white marble and exposed, not to sunlight, but to uniformly diffused light that would cast no shadows. The building would have no other apparent form than that of its contour. It would seem as flat as a great unbroken wall. Cornices, colonnades, all details, all projections within the contour lines, would disappear. The beauty of all the carefully wrought details, the fine balance and proportion of masses that had engaged the skill and enthusiasm of the designer, would vanish.

How important, then, is the consideration of the lighting of a thing designed to have light upon it—that is to say, of its shadows! As long as the sun shines on a building, its light and the shadows it casts will introduce into the design elements which to a large degree must influence the character of its details and the disposition of its masses—its handling, its style, its artistic expression. Indeed—leaving out of account considerations of construction and of the practical requirements of planning—no purely aesthetic consideration so greatly influences design as does that of shadows.

It is inevitable, therefore, that shadows should have influenced, most intimately and constantly, however gradually and unconsciously, the development of different styles of architecture in different latitudes. It is hard to imagine that the broad and simple designs of the Greeks could ever have been evolved in a northern climate where the low-lying sun would never have modeled them as does the brilliant southern sunlight for which they were intended, and where they would have seemed cold and dull.

On the other hand, can it be conceived that the cathedrals of the north of Europe could have developed naturally in Greece or Italy or Spain? There the vivid light would have cast shadows so intense as to have reduced them to an incoherent jumble of sharp lines and unyielding masses. Mystery and vastness would have disappeared and grotesqueness and violence of effect would have taken their places.

In view of these considerations the student is urged to study architectural shadows carefully and with his artistic faculties fully awake to their essential value, that he may express them quickly, readily and truly on all his studies in design, and draw and render them on his finished drawings with the greatest possible effect.

The following quotation from an article by Mr. C. Howard Walker, "The Theory of Mouldings" (*Architectural Review*, Vol. VII, No. 6, *et seq.*), bears witness to the importance of the study of shadows in connection with detail. It is needless to say that the importance of such study in relation to masses is as much greater as masses are more important than are details.

"The profile of mouldings is of minor importance compared to their relative light and shade, but as this light and shade can be obtained in various ways, much attention should be paid to the best section or profile by which to obtain it. . . . Assuming the chief characteristic of mouldings to be the beauty of contrast of light and shade . . . they require study in relation to the direction of light they receive. . . . The plane of the principal surface of the moulding is entirely influenced by the tone value of light desired. . . . In the case of wood and stone fillets, the projection is usually less than the face of the mouldings, the object of the moulding being solely to produce a line of shadow equivalent" (*i.e.*, proportional) "to the projection. . . . The head gives an entire octave of tones in light and shade, and is a moulding of higher type than the fillet, while serving the same purpose. . . . The cavetto or scotia is usually a foil to the convex mouldings or to the plane surfaces of fillets. It produces strong, effective and graded shadow, and as the major part of its surface is always in shadow, its section is seldom broken, which is not the case with the roll. . . . In some of the bases the lower tori have a peculiar cast-up form, evidently to obtain a broader shadow on the under side; they show the care with which the Greek studied the effect of mouldings."

See also Figure 1.

The Importance of the
Study of Actual Shadows

It will be of great interest and benefit to the student to observe carefully actual shadows on executed work. This observation will familiarize him with all the shadows of common architectural forms, and with those of forms less common, as well, which it would be difficult to cast with certainty unless he had a generally correct intuition of the form such shadows should take. It will increase his power of visualization—of seeing mentally how and why the shadows of an object take certain forms. It will also help him give his rendering of shadows on drawings the greatest possible interpretative force. Above all, it will train him to a just perception of the effects of actual shadows and of their relation to design; will suggest to him how to obtain those shadows that will give the effects and the proportions he desires, and how to avoid unpleasing shadow effects; and it will awaken in him, as no studies on paper can do, the perception and enjoyment of the play of light and shadow over a façade or any well-modeled object—with its subtle gradations of tone, and sharp notes of accent and contrast.

When the student has learned to see and to enjoy these effects, his work in design will take on a new spirit and vitality. For all hope of good artistic work must begin with the joy in it and in the effort to produce it.

The accompanying illustrations of the addition to the Metropolitan Museum of Fine Arts in New York, published through the courtesy of the architect, furnish a very striking example of the effects of actual shadows, and of the value of the study of shadows on drawings. The line drawing (Figure 1A) gives little foreknowledge of the effect of the executed work. It is interesting to note how much more nearly the effect of the actual building may be foreseen in the rendered drawing (Figure 1B) than in the line drawing above.

FIGURE 1A   FROM A LINE DRAWING

FIGURE 1B   FROM A RENDERED DRAWING

FIGURE 1C   FROM A PHOTOGRAPH

FIGURE 1
METROPOLITAN MUSEUM OF ART, NEW YORK CITY
RICHARD H. HUNT AND RICHARD M. HUNT, ARCHITECTS

Preliminary Suggestions as to Solutions of Problems Hereafter Given

In consideration of what has been said in the foregoing articles, the student who purposes to solve the problems given in the following treatise is asked to believe that no work required in it is not important enough to be done "in a good and workmanlike manner"; that all drawings should be accurate and clear and should have expressiveness and "quality"—that indescribable something without which any architectural work is cold and unhuman; that they should have the precision of touch of the artist, not the mere accuracy of the mechanician. Every drawing done, however simple in character, should give evidence of the architectural draftsman, of the artist; otherwise it will be entirely wide of the architectural mark.

As a help to the beginner in getting in his work the desired results, some suggestions as to methods and materials are here given.

1—A shadow should never be "guessed at." By this it is not meant that it should never be drawn without being constructed geometrically, but that it should be drawn with intuitive reasonableness and a knowledge of its form, at least—which is not "guessing." There is a great difference between the work of a draftsman who draws a shadow without constructing it, having in his mind a process of visualization and a knowledge gotten from observation and experience, and that of one who thinks that "the practical way to do these things is to guess at them" in the fullness of ignorance.

2—Instruments and materials should be in good condition and fit for their purposes. The fact that a draftsman of great skill and long experience will often make a very admirable drawing with poor instruments or materials is no reason why the beginner can do so or should attempt to do so. No good artistic work is "sloppy," though it may sometimes appear so at first to the inexperienced eye. It should be needless to say that the draftsman who does good work with poor materials does so in spite of them, not on account of them.

3—Paper. For the solution of problems, Whatman's paper, or better still, that made by the Royal British Water Colour Society, is recommended. It should be stretched on the drawing-board, which should be large enough to allow the triangles and T-square to be used readily without coming too near the edges of the board. A cheaper, calendered paper may be used if desired. It is not easy, however, to obtain on it the quality either of drawing or rendering which may be gotten on the other papers suggested; and quality is to be a prime object in every drawing.

4—Pencils. Whether or not a drawing is to be inked in before being rendered, the pencil drawing should be as good as if it were to be left in pencil. It is an almost universal delusion among young draftsmen that they can correct and improve drawings when they ink them in. The reverse is almost sure to be the result. The pen is not so tractable an instrument as the pencil. Few, if any, draftsmen can obtain the quality with it that they can with the pencil. The beginner may be sure that his inked-in drawing will not be so good as his pencil drawing.

It is all but impossible to obtain quality in a drawing done with a hard pencil. It usually takes several years of hard-earned experience for a young draftsman to become convinced of this fact. If he will but accept it on faith to begin with, he will save much of the time necessary for him to reach a given point of final development.

The hardness of the pencil to be used depends on the roughness of the paper, the moisture of the atmosphere, the skill of the draftsman, and the nature and purposes of the drawing. An experienced draftsman will lay out a drawing with an HB pencil without having the lines rub badly, where a beginner using the same pencil would have reduced the drawing to an indistinguishable blur by the time it was finished. The beginner will do well to use, on Whatman's or other rough paper, an H pencil for construction, and an F pencil for the finished lines of the object and shadows, if these lines are not to be inked in. The above grades are suggested for dry days. For damp days, when the paper is somewhat soft and spongy, pencils softer than these by about one grade will answer better. For smooth-surfaced papers use pencils about one grade softer than for Whatman's cold pressed paper. The grades referred to are those of the Hardtmuth's "Kohinoor" series.

FIGURE 2—Measured Drawing of a Window in Palazzo Communale, Bologna

By G. F. STEVENS

Keep the pencils well sharpened, with a rather long, round point—not a "chisel-point." Keep the sandpaper sharpening-block always at the elbow, and use it often enough to keep a good, sensitive point on the leads. A pianist might as well try to play with gloves on as a young draftsman to draw with a stubby point. Keep the point of the pencil well in against the edge of the T-square or triangle when drawing. Keep the pencil well down lengthwise of the line to be drawn and twist it regularly and slightly as the line is drawn. This twisting keeps the point sharp for a considerable time, and ensures a uniformity of line. Let the line have a uniform width and weight throughout its length. Let the lines be ended with a firm touch, not frayed out at the finish.

Do not be afraid to let construction lines—or even finished lines, at times—run past each other at intersections. A better touch may usually be gotten if the mind and hand are not cramped by the purpose of stopping lines at given points.

5—Do not be disturbed if the paper becomes soiled from the rubbing over the lines. While neatness is a good thing it is not good drawing. A drawing has good qualities or not quite irrespective of the cleanness of the paper it is made on. A drawing may always be inked in and washed down or cleaned with bread before being rendered, when cleanness is an object.

6—In drawing shadow lines make them not only accurately correct but as full of expression as possible. If an elevation and the shadow lines on it are well drawn, the drawing will begin to look rendered before any washes are applied. If a very light system of washes be then put on, the drawing will have a most pleasing lightness and ease of effect, as may be seen from the accompanying illustrations. (Figures 2 and 3.)

It is, of course, not intended that a much more extended and complete system of rendering is not often more appropriate than this very time-saving and knowing one. It is recommended, however, that in the solution of the problems to follow, the student render his shades and shadows with quite light flat washes, which are easiest and most quickly applied and which will not obliterate the construction lines. It will be well to leave the construction lines on the drawings.

7—In laying washes keep plenty of color on the paper and float them on. It is impossible to lay a good wash with a dry brush. Do not run over the lines to which the wash is to be brought. Force out most of the color from the brush on the edge of the color saucer before leading the wash to the line, bringing the brush to a sharp, springy point. It is, of course, assumed that the brush is a sable brush, which comes readily to a fine, elastic point.

8—The use of pure India ink is advised for the washes.

9—The system of rendering to be adopted must govern the width and depth of the shadow lines. They may, with good effect, be made quite prominent where a very light system of washes is to be used, as may be seen in Figure 3. In the following problems the student is advised not to make his shadow lines either very broad or very deep; yet they should not be wiry, nor so faint as to be lacking in decision. He will do well to surround himself with as many photographs of well-rendered drawings as possible, to which he may refer for suggestion and guidance.

10—The plates hereafter given in illustration of the text are not to be considered as models in the rendering of shadows. The requirements of the process of reproduction and the necessity of making processes of construction as clear as possible have precluded the possibility of making them also examples of good technique.

FIGURE 3

Part of the Elevation of a Court-house

By M. THIERS, Pupil of M. PASCAL

The Uses of Conventional Shadows

As noted in Article II, one of the purposes of the casting of shadows on architectural drawings is to render those drawings easy of direct interpretation. Evidently, the greatly projecting parts of a building will cast wider or deeper shadows than those parts which project less. It is also evident that the width and depth of shadows will depend upon the direction of light. That is, given a certain direction of light, the projections of parts of a building beyond other parts will be measured by the widths and depths of their shadows.

Inasmuch as the lighting of most architectural objects will be by the direct rays of the sun's light, the sun is by common convention assumed as the source of light in architectural drawings. The rays of light are therefore assumed to be parallel. Since for practical purposes the sun may be considered to be at an infinite distance, the rays of light are considered to be parallel, the convergence of its rays, which is infinitesimal for any such distances as would appear in architectural work, being neglected.

Now, if by common agreement a certain conventional direction of light be always assumed in the rendering of architectural drawings, the forms represented by those drawings may be readily interpreted from the forms and extent of the shadows which the different parts cast. Furthermore, it will be best not only to use a direction of light generally agreed upon, but a direction which will be as nearly as possible an average of different directions of sunlight. It is further evident that it will be much easier to cast shadows with certain directions of light than with others, and that it will therefore be most convenient to choose such a direction as will render the construction as simple as possible.

For all the above reasons it has been universally customary in architectural practice to consider the direction of light as being parallel to that diagonal of a cube drawn from the upper left front corner to the lower right back corner, the bottom of the cube being parallel to the ground and its front parallel to a front plane. A ray having this direction is called the "conventional ray," and will hereafter be referred to as the "ray R." (Figure 4.)

In the drawings illustrating the solutions of problems, a uniform method of lettering has been adopted with the purpose of rendering the construction as easy to follow as possible.

Points will generally be denoted by capital letters, as these are somewhat more legible than the small letters. In problems where the number of capital letters alone is insufficient, the small letters will be used in the same way as the former.

An actual point in space will be denoted by a letter, as the "point A," etc. Actual points will be thus denoted in the text, at times, when only their plans or elevations appear on the drawing.

The plan of the point A will be lettered A_1.

The shadow of point A in plan will be lettered A_{1S}.

The front elevation of A will be lettered A_2.

The shadow of A in front elevation will be lettered A_{2S}.

The side elevation of A will be lettered A_3.

The shadow of A in side elevation will be lettered A_{3S}.

The letter R will be used only to represent an actual ray having the conventional direction. Avoid confounding the ray itself with its plan and elevation which are forty-five-degree lines.

The letter r will be used only to denote the angle which the ray R makes with the horizontal and front planes.

The plane of horizontal projections will be referred to as the "plan plane" or "ground plane"; the plane of vertical projections, as the "front elevation plane," or "front plane"; the plane perpendicular to both the horizontal and front planes, as the "profile plane."

It is evident from an inspection of Figure 4, that the plan AF, the front elevation AD and the side elevation AG of the diagonal AH, or of the ray R, are all the diagonals of squares; that is to say, the plan and elevations of the ray R are forty-five-degree lines; and the ray moves equally downward, backward, and to the right. Therefore the geometrical problems involved in the casting of shadows with the conventional direction of light will be as simple as possible.

While this direction of light has become a universal convention with architects for all ordinary cases, a different direction may of course be assumed whenever necessary in specific cases. *[Article V continues on page 13]*

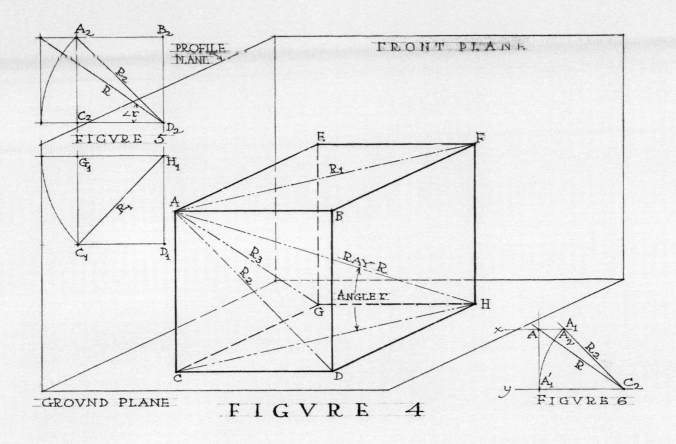

FIGVRE 5

PROFILE PLANE

FRONT PLANE

GROVND PLANE

FIGVRE 4

FIGVRE 6

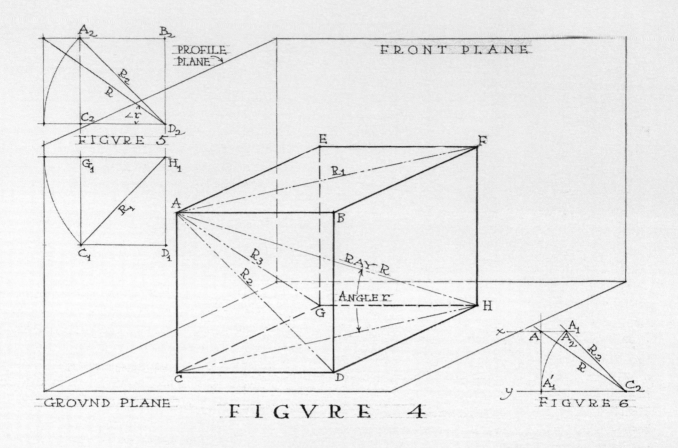

FIGVRE 4

General Methods of Casting Shadows

The true angle which ray R makes with the horizontal plane will be referred to as the angle r. It is evident from Figure 4 that this angle is to be determined as follows:

Let AB, edge of cube $= 1$.

Then $\cdot \overline{CH}^2 = \overline{CD}^2 + \overline{CG}^2 = 2\,\overline{AB}^2 = 2$

$\therefore \quad CH = \sqrt{2}$

$\therefore \quad \tan r = \dfrac{AC}{CH} = \dfrac{1}{\sqrt{2}} = .7071$

$\therefore \quad <r = 35° - 16'$

The graphical construction of r, the true angle which R makes with the horizontal plane, is shown in Figures 5 and 6, the two constructions being essentially the same. That shown in Figure 6 is the one used in practice. Through any point C_2 of a forty-five-degree line, R_2, draw a horizontal line C_2 y, and through any other point, as A_2, on the line R_2 draw a horizontal line A_2 x. With C_2 as a center and $C_2 A_2$ as a radius describe the arc $A_2 A'_1$. Erect the perpendicular A'_1 A. Then A is the position of the point A after the ray R has been revolved about C as an axis into a position where it is parallel to the front plane. Hence, $A'_1 C_2$ A is the true angle r. A comparison with Figure 5 will render the construction clear.

When a given direction of light has been agreed upon, the casting of shadows resolves itself into the problem of representing by plan and elevation the rays of light passing through the various points of the object of which the shadows are desired; and of finding where these rays are tangent to that object and where they strike the objects receiving the shadows.

As the objects themselves and the rays of light can be represented only by their plans and elevations, those plans and elevations are necessary in the solutions of problems in the determining of shades and shadows.

As intimated in the preceding article, the problem of casting shadows may be reduced to the problem of representing the rays which pass through points in the shade line of an object, and finding the points at which those rays strike another object. Generally speaking, this is not a very difficult problem in descriptive geometry, and it is one quite within the powers of an architectural draftsman of a little experience, if he will keep clearly in mind the nature of the problem he is to solve. He is apt to entangle himself in trying to remember rules and methods by which to reach a solution.

According to the character of the objects which cast or receive the shadows, however, this problem requires various methods of attack. Of these methods, four, which are those most generally applicable in dealing with architectural forms, are outlined below. They will be called:

1—*The Method of Oblique Projection.* (See Article VII.)
2—*The Method of Circumscribing Surfaces.*
(See Article VIII.)
3—*The Method of Auxiliary Shadows.* (See Article IX.)
4—*The Slicing Method.* (See Article X.)

A brief preliminary consideration of each of these here follows, and the student is urged to become thoroughly familiar with them.

The Method of Oblique Projection

This method consists simply in drawing the forty-five-degree lines representing the rays tangent to an object or passing through its shade edges, to find the points of the shade line; and in finding the points where these rays strike any other object involved in the problem. The shadow will evidently be an oblique projection of the object casting it.

It is evident from an inspection of Figure 7, that:

To find on any front plane the shadow of any point, one needs to know only the elevations of the plane and of the point, and the distance of the point in front of the plane. For, since the ray R moves equally downward, backward and to the right (Article V), the shadow A_{2S}, in elevation, of the point A will lie on the elevation of the ray passing through A—the forty-five-degree line A_2 x—and as far downward and to the right as A is from the wall. Evidently, then, the plan might have been dispensed with in determining the shadow, further than as it furnishes the distance of A from the wall. For we might have drawn the elevation, A_2 x, of the ray through A, and have taken the shadow, A_{2S}, of A on the wall, on this line at a point as far to the right or below A_2 as the point A is from the wall—the distance A_2 y.

Similarly, the shadow on a horizontal plane—in this case on the ground—of any point, B, may be determined without using the elevations except to determine the distance of B from the ground, by drawing the plan B_1 z of the ray through B, and taking the shadow B_{1S} on B_1 z at a distance back and to the right of B_1 equal to the distance of B above the ground.

The student should become thoroughly familiar with this simple and direct method which usually dispenses with the necessity of having both plan and elevation. Many of the common architectural shadows may be cast by it, and in office practice it is usually inconvenient to draw a plan of a building or object below the elevation on which shadows are to be cast. The plans and elevations are usually on different sheets and often at different scales.

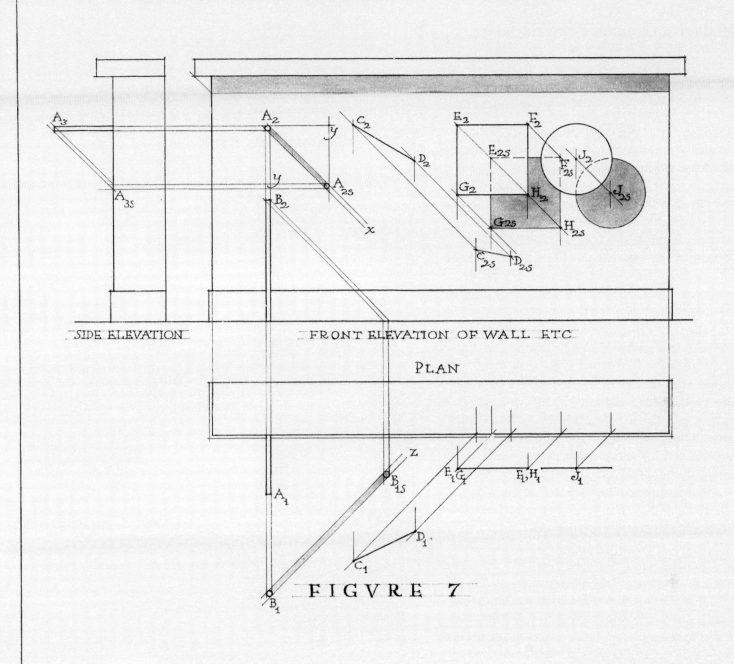

SIDE ELEVATION   FRONT ELEVATION OF WALL ETC

PLAN

FIGVRE 7

The Method of Circumscribing Surfaces

The application of this method depends on the principle that at a point of tangency of two surfaces, whatever is true of one surface is also true of the other; for such a point is common to both. If, then, we have a surface whose shade line is to be determined, and we circumscribe about this surface a tangent surface whose line of tangency and shade line are readily determined, it is evident that the point at which the shade line of the circumscribing surface crosses the line of tangency of the two surfaces will be a point of the shade line of the given surface. For, whatever is true of the circumscribing surface on the line of tangency will be true of the given surface on that line; and the point where the shade line of the former surface crosses the line of tangency of the two will be a point of the shade line of the former; therefore it will also be a point of the shade line of the latter, or given surface.

Thus in Figure 8, points A_2 and B_2 are evidently points on the shade line of the sphere. They are here supposed to be determined by the method stated above. It is easy to determine the line of tangency of the sphere and cone— in this case the horizontal line $A_2 B_2$; and the shade lines of the auxiliary cone—in this case lines $C_2 A_2$ and $C_2 B_2$ (Article XV). The intersections of the shade lines of the cone with the line of tangency at A_2 and B_2 are therefore points of the shade line of the sphere.

This method is occasionally quite convenient. It is of course applicable only to double-curved surfaces of revolution. It can be used with convenience and exactness only for finding the shades of those surfaces whose contours are arcs of circles, as it is impracticable to find accurately the lines of tangency of the auxiliary surfaces with the given surfaces unless the contours of the latter are arcs of circles. In practice, however, it is often accurate enough to assume an arc of a circle as coincident with a certain part of the contour of a given surface, even when that part is not mathematically the arc of a circle.

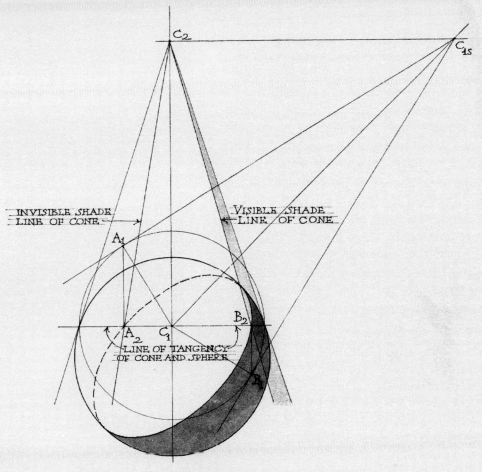

INVISIBLE SHADE
LINE OF CONE

VISIBLE SHADE
LINE OF CONE

C_2

C_{1s}

A_1

B_2

A_2 C_1

LINE OF TANGENCY
OF CONE AND SPHERE

B

FIGVRE 8

The Method of Auxiliary Shadows

The application of this method depends upon the principles that (a) if upon any surface of revolution a series of auxiliary curves be drawn, the shadow of the surface will include the shadows of all the auxiliaries, and will be tangent to those that cross the shade line of the surface, at points which are the shadows of the points of crossing; and that (b) the point of intersection of two shadow lines is the shadow of the point of intersection of those lines, if they are intersecting lines; or the shadow of the point where the shadow of one line crosses the other line, if they are not intersecting lines.

It is evident from the above that if we have the intersection of the shadows of two lines, or their point of tangency, we may pass back along the ray through the intersection or tangent point of the shadows until we arrive at the intersection or tangency of the lines casting those shadows.

The application of this method is much facilitated by the choice of auxiliary lines whose shadows may be cast as readily and as accurately as possible. It is often possible, also, to choose such a plane to receive auxiliary shadows as will simplify the construction. (Article XIV–4.)

The points above explained will be made clear by the accompanying illustration—Figure 9.

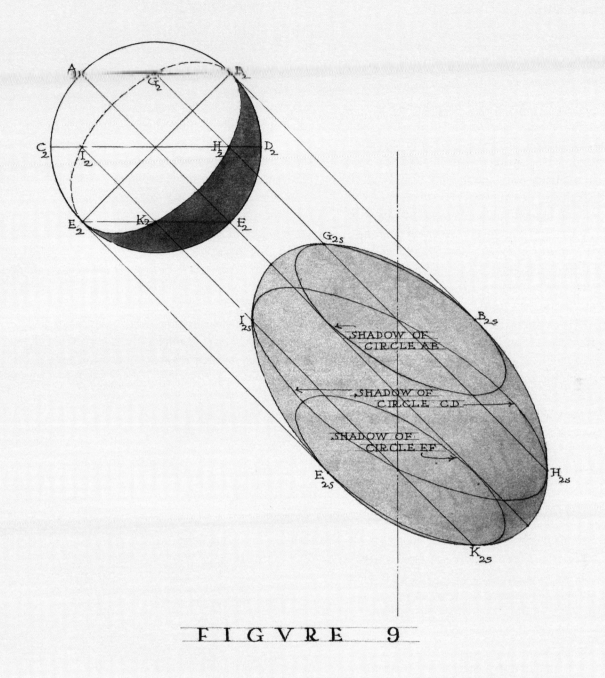

SHADOW OF
CIRCLE AB

SHADOW OF
CIRCLE CD

SHADOW OF
CIRCLE EF

FIGVRE 9

The Slicing Method

The Application of the Foregoing Methods in Practice

This method consists in (*a*) cutting through the object casting the shadow and that receiving it with vertical planes parallel to the rays of light, and (*b*) in determining points of shade and shadow by drawing rays from points in the slices cut by the auxiliary planes on the first object, to those in the slices cut on the receiving object.

The process will be sufficiently explained by Figure 10. The plans of the slicing planes are chosen at will—in this case at 1, 2, 3, 4, 5, and 6. Since the planes are vertical, the plans of the slices coincide with the plans of these planes. That is, the forty-five-degree lines—1, 2, 3, 4, 5, 6—represent the plans of the forty-five-degree slices. The elevations of these slices may now be constructed from their plans, with the aid of horizontal auxiliary circles on the surface of the scotia.

Suppose that at point 1, at the upper end of the elevation of slice 1, the elevation of a ray of light be drawn. Then the point at which the elevation of the ray crosses the elevation of the slice is a point of the shadow in elevation. For that point is on the surface of the scotia, being in a line on that surface—the slice line—and also in a ray through a point of the line which casts the shadow.

This method is very simple, and the student is often tempted to use it, on this account, where it cannot be applied to advantage. Generally it is rather difficult of application, since the construction of the slices is slow and troublesome. When points of tangency of rays to slices are involved, the method is generally not trustworthy, since there is no way of determining accurately the points of tangency. The possibility of considerable error as a result of very slight inaccuracy of construction is generally great. Of course great care in making constructions is necessary with this method. A good deal of ingenuity may be exercised in the choice of such slicing planes as will give the most valuable results and in the construction of slices in the easiest and most accurate ways.

It is plain that most architectural designs to be rendered will contain objects whose shadows cannot be cast by any one of these methods alone. Even the shadows of a single object may often be most advantageously cast by the use of several methods applied to different parts. The student is urged to exercise his ingenuity and judgment in making the most convenient special application of general principles to whatever case he may have in hand; and he is advised not to become entangled in the processes necessary in making his constructions. Some visualizing faculty and a little common sense should enable him to handle his problems well.

The problems hereafter given under Articles XXII, XXIII, and XXIV are examples of shadows where the use of more than one method is not only convenient but necessary.

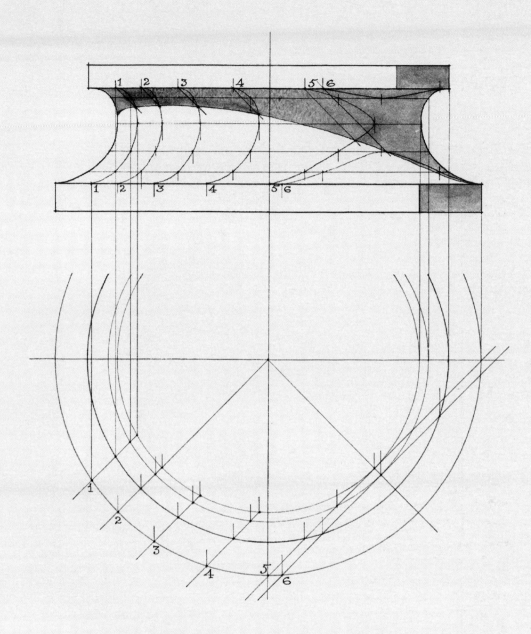

FIGVRE 10

Preliminary Considerations

A preliminary consideration of the following points will be of value:

1—*The Similarity of Problems of Shadows and those of Perspective.* Both in their nature and in principle of solution the problems of perspective and those of shadows are identical. A shadow is a projection, by rays of light, of one object on another—on a wall, for example—behind the first object with reference to the light. A perspective drawing is a projection, by rays of sight, of one object on another, the latter being usually a plane situated in front of the first object with reference to the point of sight. In the case of shadows, the shadow-picture is projected by lines of projection radiating from a source of light. In the case of perspective, the picture is projected by lines of projection radiating from the point of sight. There is no essential difference between the two. (Figures 11 and 12.)

If the point of sight in perspective be removed to an infinite distance on a line perpendicular to a front plane or plan plane, the perspective drawing becomes an elevation or plan. If the source of light be removed to an infinite distance, on a line oblique to the elevation and plan planes—the case assumed in casting shadows with sunlight—the shadow is an oblique projection.

2—In the discussions of the problems to follow, *shade* on an object will be considered as that part of it from which light is excluded by the form of the object itself. *Shadow* on an object will be that part of it from which light is excluded by some exterior object or overhanging part of the same object. The line dividing light from shade will be called the "*shade line.*" The line dividing the light from shadow will be called the "*shadow line.*" It is evident that shade lines will be determined by tangent rays, and shadow lines by incident rays.

3—*All straight lines and planes may be considered as being of indefinite extent.* Those parts of such lines and planes which lie beyond parts having actual existence in the cases considered may always be assumed. These assumed parts will be termed "*imaginary.*"

Those shade lines and shadow lines which have actual existence in cases considered will be called "*real.*" Those which have no actual existence on a given object will be called "*imaginary.*"

4—*It is evident that a point which is not in light cannot cast a real shadow.* Therefore when the shadow of an object is to be determined, let it be carefully determined, first of all, what parts of the object are in shade or shadow; for those parts can cast no real shadows. They may always cast imaginary shadows, however. *It is likewise evident that every real shade line must cast a real shadow*, since the tangent rays determining the shade line pass on, and must strike somewhere. It is also true that *this real shadow cannot lie within another real shadow*, for then it would be imaginary. Most of the time-honored blunders in the casting of shadows may be avoided by keeping these two facts clearly in mind: *that every object that is in light must cast a shadow; and that no object not in light can cast a shadow.*

5—*The line bounding the shadow of an object is really the shadow of the shade line of the object.* (Figure 11.)

6—*The shadow of a straight line on a plane may be determined by the shadows of any two of its points on the plane.*

The shadow of any line on any surface may be determined by finding the shadows of adjacent points of the line.

The shadow on a given plane of any line which is parallel to that plane is a line equal and parallel to the given line.

The shadows of parallel lines on any plane are parallel.

7—*A "plane of rays"* is the plane which may be considered as made up of the rays passing through adjacent points of a straight line.

8—The plan or side elevation of a surface can be used in finding shadows by direct projection *only when that plan or side elevation may be represented by a line.* Otherwise it is impossible to find directly points at which rays strike the given surface. Thus in the accompanying Figure 13, it is evidently easy to find the shadow, A_{2S}, of A on the cylinder, by the use of the plan. But this method cannot be used to find the shadow of B on the ovolo.

9—Since the shadow of any point must lie on the ray through that point, *the shadow in plan must always lie on the plan of the ray through the point, and its shadow in elevation must always lie on the elevation of the ray through the point.*

10—The point where the shade line of any double-curved surface of revolution touches the contour line of the surface in plan or elevation is to be found at the point of the contour at which the plan or elevation of a ray is tangent to it.

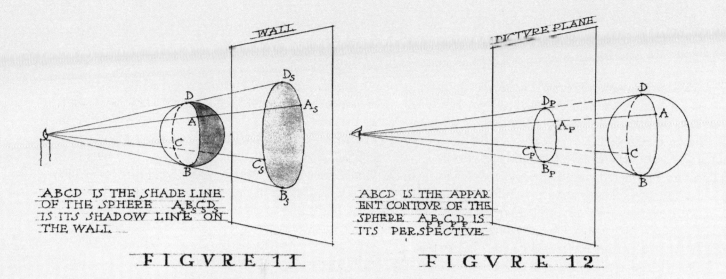

ABCD IS THE SHADE LINE
OF THE SPHERE ABCD S
IS ITS SHADOW LINE ON
THE WALL

ABCD IS THE APPAR
ENT CONTOVR OF THE
SPHERE AP BP CP DP IS
ITS PERSPECTIVE

F I G V R E 11

F I G V R E 12

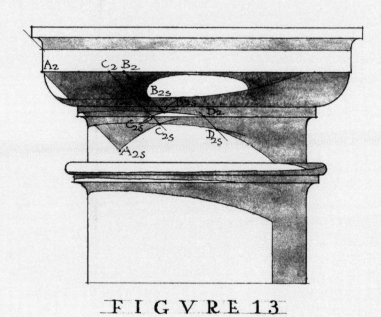

F I G V R E 13

The Shadows of Certain Straight Lines

The student will do well to become thoroughly familiar with the following shadows of straight lines on certain kinds of surfaces. That given in Section 4 will hereafter prove useful as an auxiliary—as in the shadows of the Tuscan capital. (Article XXIV.) The others recur very often in architectural drawings and are the subjects of very frequent mistakes by careless draftsmen.

1—*The Shadow of a Line Perpendicular to an Elevation Plane.* (Figure 14.) The shadow of this line in front elevation *is always a forty-five-degree line, whatever the forms of the objects receiving its shadow.* For the shadow of this line is cast by the plane of rays passing through the line, and the shadow lies in this plane; hence it will coincide in elevation with the plane of rays. But this plane of rays is perpendicular to the elevation plane, since it contains a line perpendicular to that plane; that is to say, it will be in front elevation a forty-five-degree line.

2—*The Shadow in Plan of a Line Perpendicular to the Plan Plane.* The explanation given above will indicate the reasoning by which this shadow is shown to be a forty-five-degree line.

3—*The Shadow of a Vertical Line on a Plane whose Horizontal Lines are Parallel to the Elevation Plane, such as a Roof Plane in Front Elevation.* (Figure 15.) This shadow is an inclined line whose slope is equal to that of the given plane. The construction shown in Figure 15 will make this clear.

4—*The Shadows of Horizontal Lines Parallel and Perpendicular to the Elevation Plane, on a Vertical Plane sloping Backward and to the Left at an Angle of Forty-five Degrees.* (Figure 16.) As shown by the construction in Figure 16, these shadows are forty-five-degree lines sloping downward to the left and right respectively.

These shadows and the plane receiving them are often useful as auxiliaries, as will appear hereafter, as, for example, in the case of the Tuscan capital. (Article XXIV.)

5—*The Shadow of a Vertical Line on a Series of Horizontal Mouldings Parallel to a Front Plane.* (Figure 17.) The vertical line is in this case $A_1 B_1$ in plan and $A_2 B_2$ in elevation. It is evident that the shadow of AB on the horizontal mouldings behind it is the line cut on the face of those mouldings by a plane of rays passing through AB. The plan of this plane is $A_1 Y_1$, and the plan of the line which it cuts on the mouldings is A_{1S}, D_{1S}. Now in plan a is equal to b. That is, the front elevation of the shadow line, $A_{2S} C_{2S} D_{2S} B_{2S}$, is equal to the profile of the right section of the mouldings.

It is true, then, that the shadow in front elevation of any vertical line on any series of horizontal mouldings or surfaces parallel to a front plane is the same as the contour of those surfaces or mouldings; and that *the shadow line moves to the right as the contour recedes.*

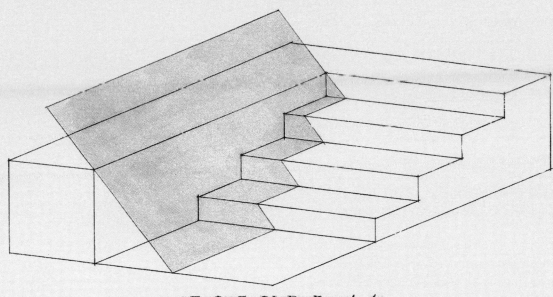

FIGVRE 14

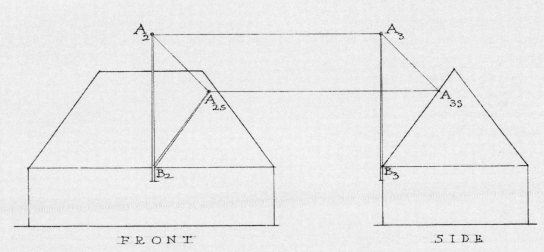

FRONT   SIDE

FIGVRE 15

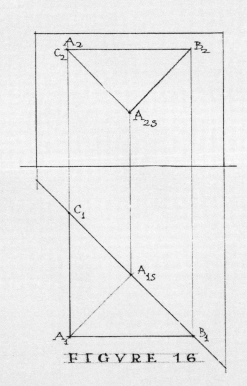

FIGVRE 16

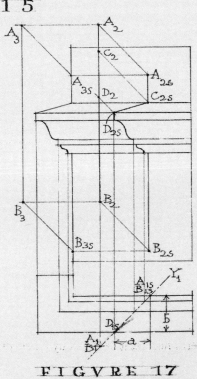

FIGVRE 17

The Shadows of Circles

Rays through adjacent points of a circle form a cylinder of rays which casts the shadow of the circle. As the section of any cylinder cut by any plane oblique to its axis is an ellipse, it follows that the shadow of any circle on any such plane is an ellipse. If the plane be parallel to the circle, the shadow will of course be a circle—which is an ellipse of special form.

In the case of the shadow of the circle on a plane parallel to its own plane, that shadow is an equal circle (Article XII-6) whose center is in the ray through the center of the given circle.

In other cases, the most convenient and accurate method of finding the shadow is to find the shadow of the square or of the octagon circumscribed about the given circle, and then to inscribe within these auxiliaries the ellipse of shadow of the circle. If the shadow is to be cast on an oblique plane, it will sometimes be inconvenient to find the shadow of the circumscribing octagon, and in such cases it will usually be accurate enough to cast the shadow of the circumscribing square only. If the shadow is to be cast on an elevation or plan plane, however, it is quite easy to cast the shadow of the circumscribing octagon, and as it is much more accurate to use it in the construction than the square alone, it is always best to do so.

The accompanying Figure 18 gives the construction for three common cases; that of a circle parallel to a wall, that of one perpendicular to a wall and parallel to the plan plane, and that of one perpendicular to a wall and to the plan plane. *[Article XIV continues on page 29]*

FIGVRE 18

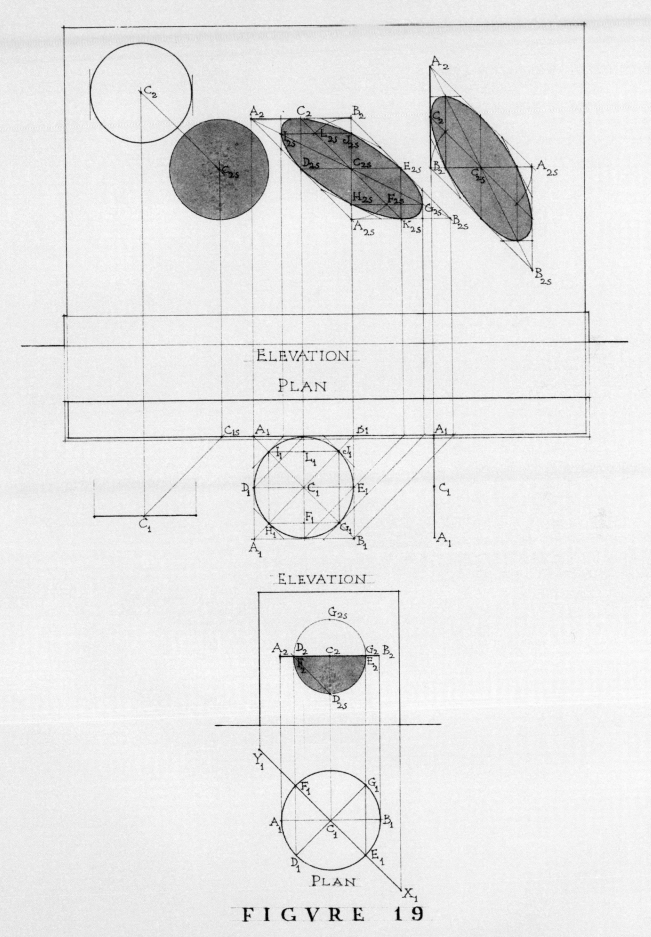

ELEVATION

PLAN

ELEVATION

PLAN

FIGVRE 19

FIGVRE 18

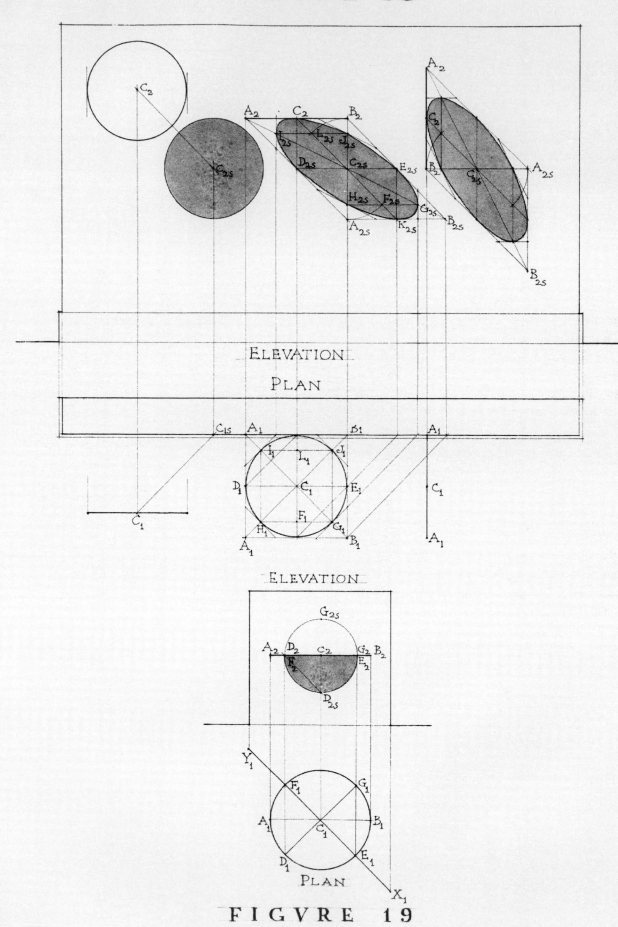

ELEVATION

PLAN

ELEVATION

PLAN

FIGVRE 19

The use of the plans in these cases was not at all necessary. The plans are shown here merely to render the reasoning of the solution more intelligible. In practice, the plans would never be used.

1—*The Shadow of a Circle Parallel to a Wall which is Parallel to the Elevation Plane.* (Figure 18.) In this case it is only necessary to find the shadow of the center. With this point as a center and a radius equal to that of the given circle, we may then describe the circle of shadow. The shadow of the center of the given circle is of course found on the elevation of the ray through the center, and at a distance to the right and downward equal to the distance of the center from the wall; that is to say, at C_{2S}, a distance along the forty-five-degree line $C_2 C_{2S}$ equal to the diagonal of a square of which the distance of C from the wall is the side.

2—*The Shadow of a Circle whose Plane is Parallel to the Plan Plane and Perpendicular to the Elevation Plane.* (Figure 18.) First cast the shadow of the circumscribing square AA BB. This shadow is $A_2 A_{2S} B_{2S} B_2$. The diagonals and median line of the shadow of the square are then drawn. The medians give the points of tangency C_2, K_{2S}, D_{2S}, E_{2S}.

It is evident from an inspection of the plan that if we can determine the shadow of F on the shadow of CF, we can readily find the shadows of H and G by drawing through the shadow of F the shadow of GH to its intersection with the shadows of the diagonals. It is further evident that, having determined the shadows of H, G, etc., we may readily draw the tangents to the curve at those points, since they will be parallel to the shadows of diagonals. These tangents will aid greatly in drawing the shadow accurately.

Now the shadow of F lies at F_{2S} on $C_{2S} K_{2S}$, at a distance from C_{2S} equal to the diagonal of a square whose side is the distance of F in front of C. Since this diagonal is $C_1 G_1$, the radius of the circle, it is easy to determine F_{2S} and L_{2S} as indicated on the drawing, without reference to the plan, and hence to determine the shadows of the circumscribing octagon.

3—*The Shadow on a Wall Parallel to the Elevation Plane, of a Circle Perpendicular to the Wall and to the Plan Plane.* (Figure 18.) The method of construction in this case is exactly the same as for the preceding, and need not be here given in detail.

Every draftsman should be so familiar with the forms of the shadows of the three circles given in Figure 18 that he can draw them from memory with reasonable accuracy.

All three forms occur frequently in practice. The shadows of an arcade on a wall behind it involve the first and third cases. See, for example, the arcade shown in Figure 40. The second case, that of a circle parallel to the plan plane and perpendicular to the elevation plane, is exemplified in Figures 42, 43, 46, 49, etc.

4—*The Shadow of a Circle Parallel to the Plan Plane, on a Vertical Plane Passing through the Center of the Circle Backward to the Left at an Angle of Forty-Five Degrees with the Front Plane.* (Figure 19.) The plan of the circle is $A_1 E_1 G_1$. The plan of the plane is $X_1 Y_1$. The elevation of the circle is $A_2 B_2$. It is evident that the shadow in elevation of the circle on XY is the circle $D_2 D_{2S} G_2 G_{2S}$, having the center C as its center, and a radius equal to the elevation of the forty-five-degree radius, CE, of the given circle. For this shadow is an ellipse, one of whose axes is $F_2 E_2$, and whose other axis is the shadow of DG. (See plan.) But this shadow in elevation, $C_2 D_{2S}$, is equal to $C_2 F_2$. That is, the semi-major and semi-minor axes of the ellipse of shadow being equal, the ellipse is a circle whose radius is $C_2 E_2$ or $C_2 F_2$.

This shadow is often very useful as an auxiliary, and the student should become familiar with the use of it in the solution of problems given hereafter, as in the case of the shadows of the Tuscan capital. (Article XXIV.)

The Shades and Shadows of Cones

The shadow of any cone on any plane may be determined by casting the shadow of the base of the cone and the shadow of its apex on the plane, and drawing shadow lines from the shadow of the apex tangent to the shadow of the base. These two latter lines will be the shadows of the shade lines of the cone. The points at which these two shadow lines are tangent to the shadow of the base are the shadows of the points at which the shade lines of the cone meet its base. (Article IX–*b*.) Hence the shade lines may be determined by passing back along the rays through these two tangent points to the points on the base which are the feet of the shade lines, and drawing the shade lines from the points thus determined to the apex. (Figure 20.)

If the plane be that of the base of the cone, the shadow of the base on that plane will coincide with the base, and it will be only necessary to cast the shadow of the apex on that plane to determine the shade and shadow of the cone, as indicated in Figure 20. This is the method most convenient in practice.

It is evident that the exact points of tangency, B and C (Figure 20), can be conveniently determined with precision only when the base of the cone lying in the plane is a circle.

Figure 21 shows the construction for determining the shade lines of a cone whose base is circular and whose axis is perpendicular to the plane of the base.

Figure 22 shows the construction for determining the shadow lines of the same cone inverted. In this case, the rays passing downward will not cast the shadow of the apex on the plane of the base. It is evident, however, that rays passing in a direction opposite to that of R will be tangent to the cone at the same points as would rays having the direction R. We may then cast the shadow of the apex on the plane of the base with a ray having the direction opposite to R. The construction is similar to that shown for the upright cone.

From the constructions shown in Figure 23 and Figure 24, it is evident (*a*) that a cone with a vertical axis and a circular right section will have no visible shade in elevation when its contour elements make an angle of forty-five degrees or less with the horizontal line of the base; and that when these elements make the angle forty-five degrees, the shade in plan is a quarter circle; and (*b*) that when these elements make the angle r or a less angle with the horizontal, the cone has no shade and no shadow on the plane of the base.

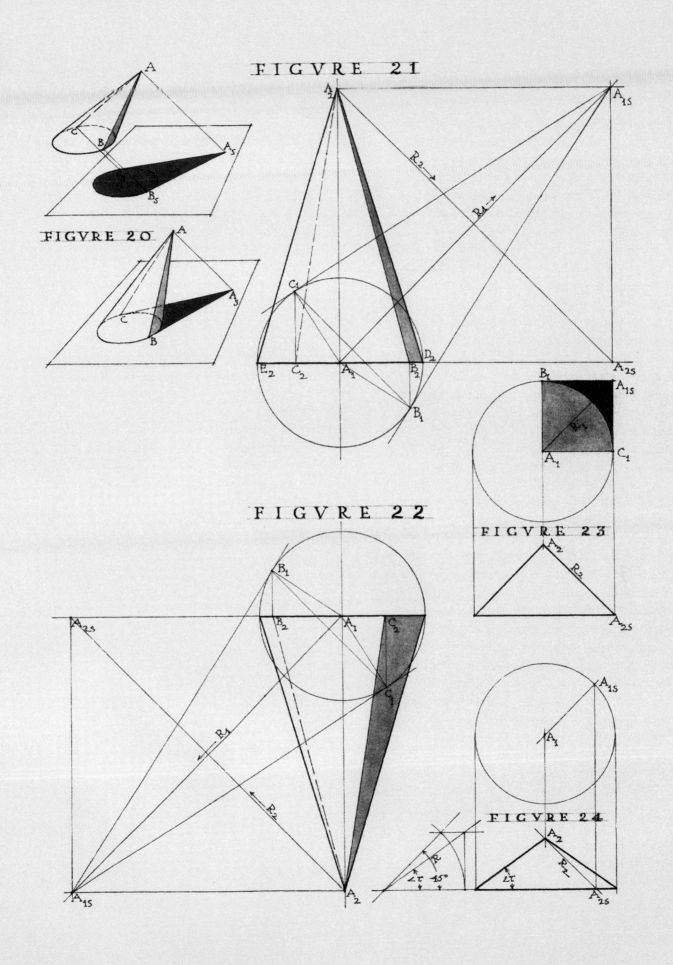

FIGVRE 21

FIGVRE 20

FIGVRE 22

FIGVRE 23

FIGVRE 24

The Shades and Shadows of Cylinders

The general principles involved in the determination of the shades and shadows of cylinders are the same as those involved in finding the shades and shadows of cones.

1—*The Shadow of any Cylinder on any Plane.* (Figure 25.) Let ABCD be any cylinder, and EF any plane. To cast the shadow of the cylinder on the plane, cast the shadows of the bases of the cylinder on the plane at $A_S B_S$ and $C_S D_S$. Draw lines $A_S C_S$ and $B_S D_S$ to complete the shadow. $A_S C_S$ and $B_S D_S$ are the shadows of the shade lines of the cylinder. Hence we may pass back along the rays through the points of tangency, A_S, B_S, C_S and D_S, to the ends of the shade lines, A, B, C and D. It is evident that a plane of rays can be tangent to the cylinder only along an element of the cylinder. Hence the shade lines of a cylinder will always be parallel to its profile lines both in plan and in elevation.

2—*The Shadow of a Cylinder on the Plane of one of its Bases.* (Figure 26.) If one base of the cylinder lies in the plane, as in Figure 26, its shadow on that plane will coincide with itself, and to find the shadow of the cylinder it will be necessary to cast only the shadow of the other base on the plane and draw shadow lines tangent to the base lying in the plane and to the shadow of the other base. From the points of tangency of these shadow lines with the base draw the shade lines parallel to the profile elements of the cylinder. Here the upper base of the cylinder is the circle whose center is C. The shadow of this center on the plane of the lower base is at C_{1S}. Then the shadow of the upper base on this plane is the circle $A_{1S} B_{1S}$. The shadow of the lower base on its own plane coincides with this base, and is in plan the circle $E_1 D_1$. We may now complete the shadow by drawing $A_{1S} D_1$ and $B_{1S} E_1$ tangent to the two base shadows. The points of tangency E_1 and D_1 give the plans of the lower ends of the shade lines. From these plans we determine the elevations at E_2 and D_2. From E_2 and D_2 we draw the shade lines in elevation parallel to the profile elements of the cylinder.

3—*The Shadow of an Upright Cylinder.* (Figure 27.) The case which occurs oftenest in architectural drawing is that of a cylinder with a vertical axis and circular right section. Since in this case the elements of the cylinder are all vertical the shade lines will be vertical, and the tangent planes of rays will be vertical planes whose plans will be forty-five-degree lines tangent to the circle of the base. The points of tangency of these planes in plan determine the plans of the shade lines, from which the elevations of these lines are drawn. The exact points of tangency should, of course, be determined, not by drawing the tangents, but by drawing the diameter normal to them—$C_1 A_1$; for the exact point of tangency of a line to a circle is determined by drawing the radius normal to the given line.

It will be convenient to remember that *the visible shade line $A_2 A_2$ is nearly one-sixth of the diameter from the right profile line.*

It should be noted that the shadow of such a cylinder—a column, for example—on a front plane has *a greater width than the diameter of the column.* The width of the shadow is equal to the diagonal of a square whose side is the diameter of the column.

[Article XVI continues on page 35]

FIGVRE 25

FIGVRE 26

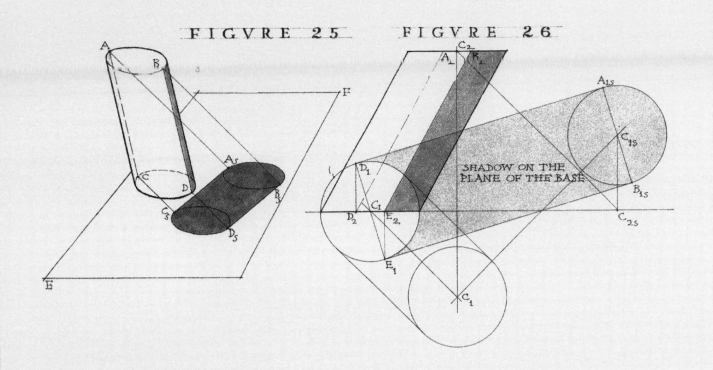

SHADOW ON THE
PLANE OF THE BASE

FIGVRE 27

FIGVRE 28

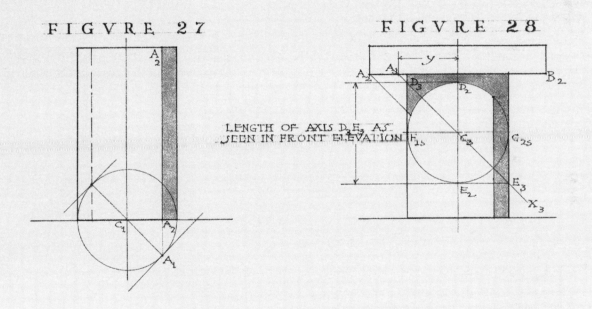

LENGTH OF AXIS D_2E_2 AS
SEEN IN FRONT ELEVATION F_{1s}

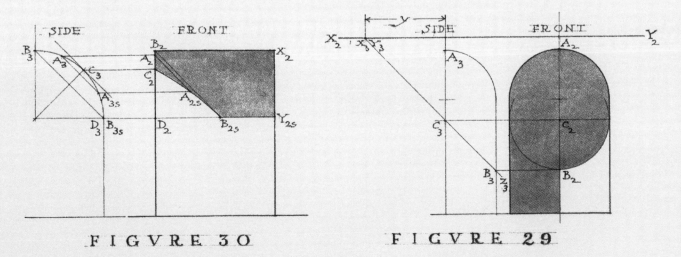

SIDE   FRONT

SIDE   FRONT

FIGVRE 30

FIGVRE 29

FIGVRE 25

FIGVRE 26

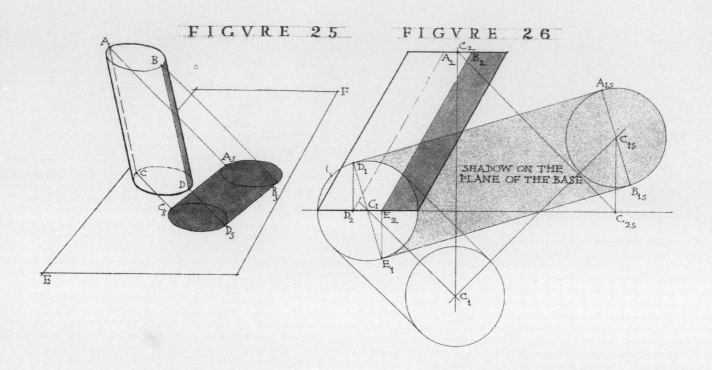

SHADOW ON THE
PLANE OF THE BASE

FIGVRE 27

FIGVRE 28

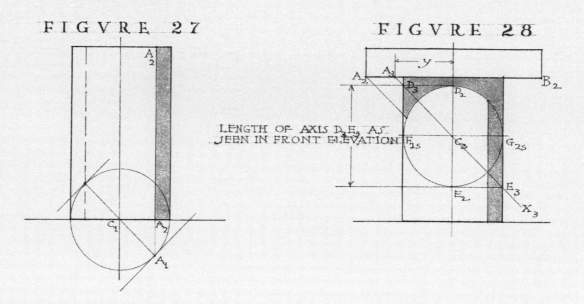

LENGTH OF AXIS $D_2 E_2$ AS
SEEN IN FRONT ELEVATION

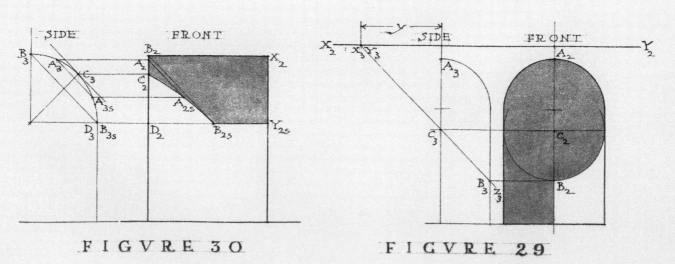

SIDE   FRONT

SIDE   FRONT

FIGVRE 30

FIGVRE 29

4—*The Shadow of a Horizontal Line Parallel to the Elevation Plane on a Cylinder of Circular Section and Vertical Axis.* (Figure 28.) This shadow is a semicircle, whose center is in the axis of the cylinder at a distance below the given line equal to the distance of the given line in front of the axis. In this case, the line is in front elevation $A_2 B_2$, at a distance Y in front of the axis. Then the side elevation of the line is A_3, the side elevation of the cylinder being the same as the front. It is evident that the shadow of AB is cast by a plane of rays whose profile in side elevation is the forty-five-degree line $A_3 X_3$; that this plane cuts the line of shadow on the cylinder, which in side elevation is $D_3 E_3$; that this line is an ellipse whose major axis is $D_3 E_3$ and whose minor axis is the diameter of the cylinder; that in front elevation this major axis is $D_2 E_2$, which is the diameter of the cylinder. Hence the major and minor axes of the ellipse of shadow being equal in front elevation, the shadow is a circle in this elevation. It is also evident that C_3, the center of this circle, is as far below AB as AB is in front of the axis.

5—*The Shadow of a Horizontal Line Parallel to the Elevation Plane on the Cylindrical Part of a Semicircular Niche.* (Figure 29.) Similar reasoning will show that this is also a semicircle struck from a center, C_2, on the axis of the niche at a distance below the line XY equal to the distance y of that line in front of the axis.

6—*The Shadow of a Cylindrical Barrel-Vault in Section.* (Figure 30.) The shadow of B, the highest point of the face line of the vault which casts the shadow $C_2 A_{2S} B_{2S}$, is at B_{2S} on the horizontal line at the level of the springing of the vault. The part CD of the face line will evidently cast no shadow, and the shadow of BC will begin at C_2. The curve of shadow $C_2 A_{2S} B_{2S}$ will be tangent at B_{2S} to the elevation, $B_2 B_{2S}$, of the ray through B. If necessary, intermediate points of the shadow line, as A_{2S}, may be found from side elevation. The shadow of BX will, of course, be the horizontal line $B_{2S} Y_{2S}$.

Cylindrical forms appear in architectural work more frequently, perhaps, than do any other geometrical curved surfaces. Such forms are exemplified in the niche, Figures 31 and 32; in the circular tower, Figure 42; in the column, with the cinctures at the base, Figure 43; in the building with circular plan, seen in section, Figure 52; in barrel-vaults; in the soffits of arches, and the like. Some of these are covered cylinders, and others concave; but there is no difference in the principles to be applied in determining the shades and shadows in these different cases, with all of which the draftsman should become thoroughly familiar.

The Shadow of a Circular Niche with a Spherical Head

$L_1 L_2 K_2 M_2 M_1$ is the front elevation of a niche and $L_1 L_{1S} M_1$ is its plan. It is evident that the part $H_2 M_2 M_1$ of the face line will not cast a shadow on the surface of the niche. The shadows of points of the part $H_2 K_2$ cannot be found by direct projection because it is impossible to represent the surface of the spherical head by a line. (Article XII–9.) We proceed, therefore, to find the shadows of these points on the spherical part of the niche by the method of auxiliary shadows. (Article IX.)

1—Let $W_1 X_1$ and $Y_1 Z_1$ be the plans of two vertical planes parallel to the face of the niche. Since these planes are parallel to the face line of the niche, the shadows of that line on these planes are readily found. It is only necessary to cast the shadows, C_{2S}, of C on these planes, and with those points as centers to strike the shadows, that is, circles 1 and 2. It is not necessary to draw the whole of each of these auxiliary shadows.

2—The planes WX and YZ also cut from the niche the lines $E_1 F_2 G_2$ and $A_1 B_2 D_2$.

3—Now every point on $E_1 F_2 G_2$ and on $A_1 B_2 D_2$ is in the surface of the niche, and every point on circles 1 and 2 is in the shadow of the face line of the niche. Hence the intersection of $E_1 F_2 G_2$ with circle 2, and that of $A_1 B_2 D_2$ with circle 1, must be points of the shadow line of the niche.

4—Evidently those points whose shadows fall on the cylindrical part of the niche, such as K, may have their shadows cast directly, since the cylinder may be represented in plan by a line, $L_1 L_{1S} M_1$.

5—The shadow line is tangent to the face line of the niche at H_2. This fact is often forgotten.

6—The shadow line is tangent to the elevation of the axis $C_1 C_2$ at L_{2S}. This is also often forgotten.

7—In practice the shadow line may be found quite accurately enough for drawings at small scale by finding the points H_2, L_{2S}, and K_{2S}, and drawing the shadow through these three points, tangent to $M_2 H_2 K_2$ at H_2, and to the axis at L_{2S}. K_{2S} may be taken on the elevation of the ray CK at a distance from C_2 a trifle more than one-third of the length of the radius $C_2 M_2$.

If the niche has a different form or position from those here given, other methods which are suited to the particular case may be adopted. Figure 32 shows the shadows in the heads of the first two flutes to the right of the axis of a Corinthian column, found by the slicing method. (Article X.)

FIGVRE 31

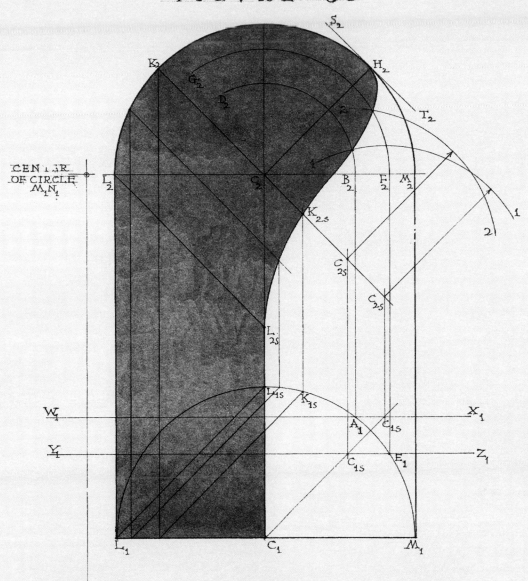

FIGVRE 32

The Shades and Shadows of Spheres

Figure 33 shows the plan and elevation of any sphere.

1—To find the shade line in plan.

The shade line will be a great circle of the sphere, which will be an ellipse in both plan and elevation. The plan will be an ellipse whose axes are $A_1 B_1$ and $D_1 E_1$. The length of the major axis is evidently that of the diameter of the sphere, $A_1 B_1$.

2—The plans of the shade points lying on the equator of the sphere are determined by the points of tangency of two vertical planes of rays, whose plans are $W_1 X_1$ and $Y_1 Z_1$. (Article XII–10.) The points in plan are A_1 and B_1, which are exactly and easily determined by drawing the diameter $A_1 B_1$ normal to the planes $W_1 X_1$ and $Y_1 Z_1$. The elevations of these points are then found on the elevation of the equator at A_2 and B_2. A_2 and B_2 might have been found directly on the elevation by drawing the forty-five-degree diameter $F_2 G_2$, and projecting points A_2 and B_2 to the equator from F_2 and G_2.

3—Now since the ellipses of shade in plan and in elevation will be symmetrical on axes $A_1 B_1$ and $H_2 I_2$ respectively, points M_1, N_1, O_1, and P_1 in plan, and A_2, K_2, B_2, and J_2 in elevation, may readily be determined by the symmetrical construction shown.

4—Points at the extremities of the minor axes of the ellipses may be determined by the intersection of these axes by thirty-degree lines drawn from the extremities of the major axes. The geometrical proof of this is given below in Section 6.

5—Figure 34 shows the plan and elevation of the shade and the shadow on a horizontal plane after the sphere and rays have been revolved until the rays are parallel to a front plane. From the similarity of the triangles $A_2 B_2 D_2$ and $A_2 B_2 A_{2S}$, it will be seen that the ellipse of a shadow in plan will circumscribe two equilateral triangles whose bases are in the minor axis of the ellipse, which is equal to the diameter of the sphere and is perpendicular to the rays in plan, and whose vertices are at the extremities of the major axis of the ellipse. For—

$$\frac{A_{2S} B_2}{A_2 B_2} = \frac{A_2 B_2}{A_2 D_2}$$

But $A_{2S} B_{2S} = A_{1S} B_{1S}$ = major axis of the shadow-ellipse

and $A_2 B_2$ = diameter of sphere = major axis of shade-ellipse

$\qquad\qquad$ = minor axis of shadow-ellipse

and $A_2 D_2 = A_1 B_1$ = minor axis of shade-ellipse.

Hence $\dfrac{A_{1S} B_{1S}}{\text{diameter}} = \dfrac{\text{diameter}}{A_1 B_1}$

or, $\dfrac{\text{major axis of shadow-ellipse}}{\text{minor axis of shadow-ellipse}} = \dfrac{\text{major axis of shade-ellipse}}{\text{minor axis of shade-ellipse}}$

That is, the axes of the ellipse of shadow bear the same relation to each other as do the axes of the ellipse of shade. And, as noted above, the ellipse of shade circumscribes two equilateral triangles whose bases are the minor axis of the ellipse and whose vertices are at the extremities of the major axis.

The axes of the ellipse of shadow intersect at the shadow of the center of the sphere.

The shadow of the sphere on a front plane is evidently to be found in the same way as above described.

Therefore, to cast the shadow of a sphere on a plan plane or front plane, cast the shadow of the center of the sphere on that plane; through this point draw the axes of the ellipse of shadow, the minor axis being perpendicular to the direction of the rays and equal to the diameter of the sphere; on the minor axis as a base construct two equilateral triangles, and about these circumscribe the shadow line.

It is not important that the student should remember the reasoning giving the proofs in the foregoing sections, or that in the following section 6. It will suffice for him to remember simply the method of constructing the shades and shadows of the sphere.

6—To determine the extremities of the minor axis of the shade line by determining the angle which the lines drawn to them from the extremities of the major axis make with the major axis. (Figure 33.)

In the plan $A_1 E_1 B_1$ of the shade line, draw lines $A_1 E_1$ and $B_1 E_1$. It is desired to determine the angle $E_1 A_1 C_1$.

Revolve the shade line about AB as an axis until it is horizontal, coinciding in plan with $A_1 E'_1 B_1$. Then the revolved position of O_1 is O'_1; of E_1 is E'_1; of $A_1 E_1$ is $A_1 E'_1$. Then $A_1 E'_1 C_1$ is one-half of a square. Through O'_1 draw $O'_1 S_1$, parallel to $A_1 E'_1$. Then $S_1 Q_1 O'_1$ is one-half of a square, and triangle $A_1 O'_1 C_1$ is equilateral.

If now the shade line be revolved back to its original position, $A_1 E_1 B_1$, $A_1 E_1$ will be parallel to $S_1 O_1$, the revolved position of $S_1 O'_1$.

Now in triangles $S_1 O_1 Q_1$ and $O'_1 A_1 Q_1$, $A_1 Q_1 = O_1 Q_1$ and $O'_1 Q_1 = S_1 Q_1$. Hence angle $O_1 S_1 Q_1$ = angle $A_1 O'_1 Q_1 = 30^\circ$. Hence the angle $E_1 A_1 C_1$ is thirty degrees.

Then the shade lines of a sphere in plan and elevation are ellipses, each circumscribing two equilateral triangles whose bases are the minor axes of the ellipses, and whose vertices are at the extremities of the major axes, which are equal to the diameter of the sphere.

The minor axes coincide in direction with the rays in plan and elevation respectively, and the major axes are respectively perpendicular to the direction of the rays.

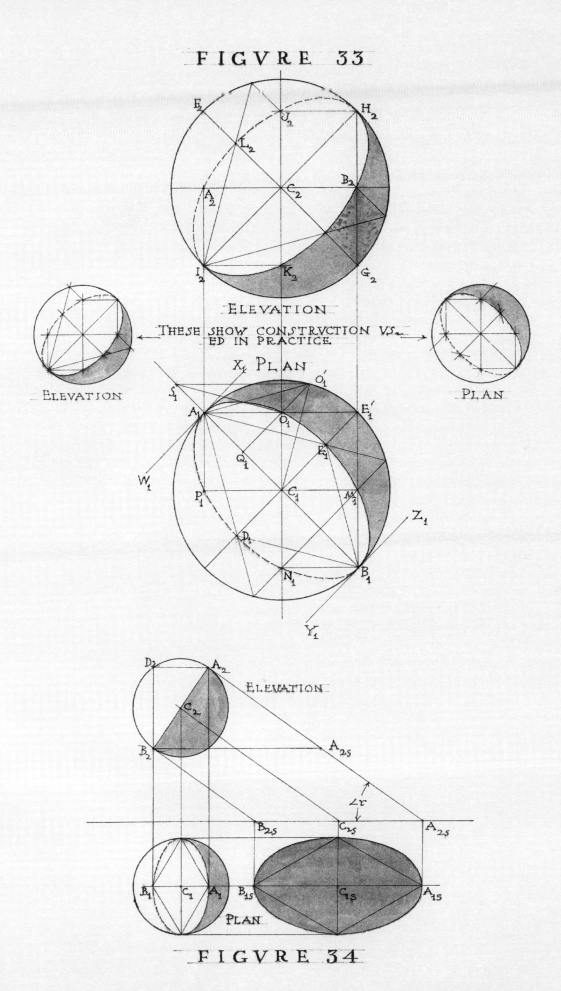

FIGVRE 33

ELEVATION

THESE SHOW CONSTRVCTION VS ED IN PRACTICE.

X_1 PLAN

ELEVATION

PLAN

ELEVATION

PLAN

FIGVRE 34

The Shadows of Dormers, Chimneys, Etc., on Roofs

The Shadows of Dormers on Roofs. (Figures 35 and 36.)
To find the shadow of any point, as A, on the roof (Figure 35), it is only necessary to find the point where the ray through A strikes the roof. Since the roof is an inclined plane whose plan cannot be represented by a line, we use in this case the side elevation, in which the plane of the roof is represented by the line $X_3 Y_3$. The side elevation of the ray through A is $A_3 A_{3S}$, and the side elevation of the shadow is A_{3S}. From A_{3S} we pass along the level line $A_{3S} A_{2S}$ to the front elevation A_{2S} of the shadow, on the front elevation $A_2 A_{2S}$ of the ray. The shadow of any other point may be cast in the same way.

It is advisable, of course, to cast the shadows on the object itself before proceeding to cast the shadow of the object on the roof. For example, it will be evident in this case, when the shadows have been cast on the dormer, that CD does not cast shadow, and that the shadow $C_{2S} B_{2S}$ is cast by BC.

It is clear from the construction that (*a*) the points at which the rays through various given points strike the roof in side elevation, give the *levels* of the shadows of those points in front elevation; (*b*) that the shadow of the eaves line AE—which is, in front elevation, a line perpendicular to the elevation plane—is a forty-five-degree line (Article XIII–1); (*c*) that the shadow $F_{2S} G_{2S}$ of FG, which is a horizontal line parallel to the roof, will be a horizontal line parallel to FG; (*d*) that the shadow $F_{2S} H_{2S}$, in front elevation, of FH, which is a perpendicular line, has the same slope as the roof (Article XIII–3).

Figure 36 shows the shadow of a dormer with a hip-roof. The method of obtaining the shadow is the same as that given above.

Shadows of Chimneys on Roofs. (Figure 37.)
The method here used is the same as that used in the preceding cases of shadows of dormers, and needs no further comment.

In dealing with objects which have the same contour in side as in front elevation, it is generally unnecessary to draw a side elevation of the object when the front elevation may be used for the side. By simply drawing on the front elevation a line representing the side elevation of the roof, wall, or whatever contour plane is involved, in such position with reference to the profile of the object as it would have in side elevation, the front may be made to do duty as a side elevation. The draftsman should become apt at using such time-saving devices whenever possible. For example, let us suppose that the depth of the chimney shown in Figure 37 is two-thirds of its width. Through A_2 draw $X_3 Y_3$, making angle $Y_3 A_2 B_2$ equal to the slope of the roof on which the shadow is to be cast. Then $X_3 Y_3$ will represent the side elevation of the roof and $A_2 D_2 C_2 E_3 F_3 G_2$ will represent the side elevation of the chimney, $A_2 D_2 C_2$ representing its front face.

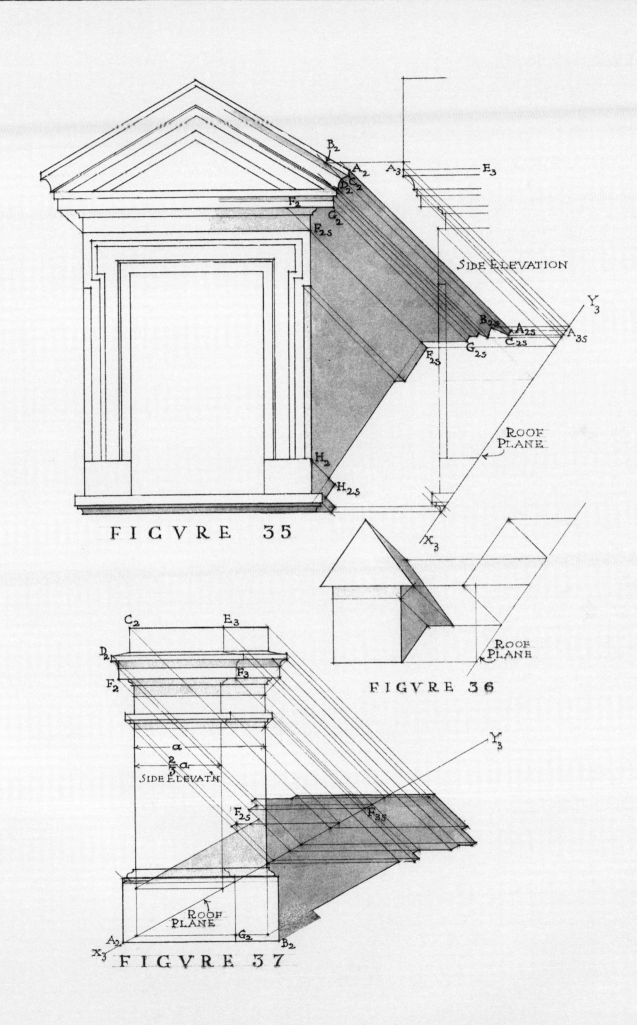

B_2
A_2
A_3
E_3
C_2
D_2
F_2
G_2
F_{2S}

SIDE ELEVATION

B_{2S}
A_{2S}
A_{3S}
G_{2S}
C_{2S}
Y_3

F_{2S}

ROOF PLANE

H_2
H_{2S}

X_3

FIGVRE 35

ROOF PLANE

FIGVRE 36

C_2
E_3
D_2
F_2
F_3

a
$\tfrac{2}{3}a$
SIDE ELEVAT'N

Y_3

F_{2S}
F_{3S}

ROOF PLANE

A_2
G_2
B_2
X_3

FIGVRE 37

The Shadows on Steps

The Shadow of a Raking Buttress on a Flight of Steps.
(Figure 38.)

Here it is convenient to use the side elevations of the buttress and of the planes of the steps, though these objects might be represented in plan by lines.

Assume the side elevation of the front face of the buttress to be A_3 G_3 I_3. Then assume the position of the profile of the steps with reference to the front face of the buttress. In this case, the profile of the steps is the line K_{3S} I_{3S} H_{3S} G_{3S}, etc. The side elevation of the right side of the raking top of the buttress, which here casts shadow, is now drawn at A_3 D_3 G_3, etc.

We may now proceed to cast the shadows by direct projection, exactly as in the preceding article.

By drawing the rays from the upper and lower corners of any riser, as E_{3S} F_{3S}, back to the buttress lines, we may determine just what part of the edge of the buttress casts shadow on any step. In this case, the part whose side elevation is E_3 F_3 casts the shadow E_{3S} F_{3S} in side elevation, which is the shadow E_{2S} F_{2S} in front elevation.

It is evident that since the raking edge of the buttress is similarly situated with reference to all the steps which receive its shadow, and has the same direction with reference to them all, the shadow of that edge on one step, as E_{2S} F_{2S}, may be repeated on the others without being cast.

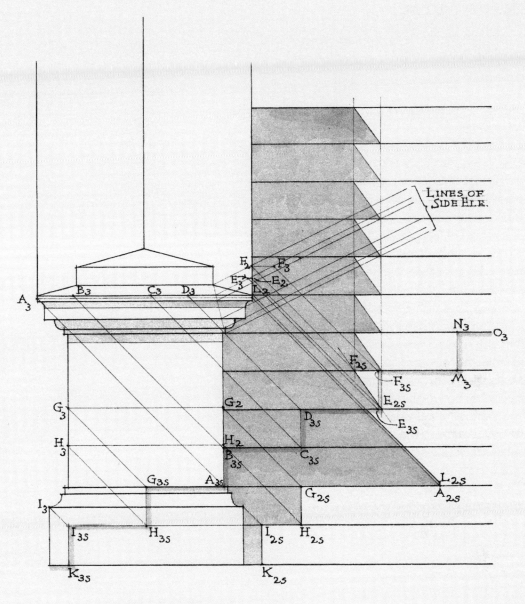

LINES OF SIDE ELE.

FIGVRE 38

The Shadows on Steps

The Shadows of a Square Buttress and Lamp on a Flight of Steps. (Figure 39.)

The casting of the shadows in this case does not involve any principles or methods other than those previously cited.

Since the lamp would surely be placed on the buttress at the same distance from the front as from the sides, no plan is needed. The side elevation is represented by the front elevation on which is placed the profile line of steps A_{3S} B_{3S} C_{3S}, etc., in right relation to the left side of the lamp and buttress, which will then represent the side elevation of the front of the lamp and buttress.

Rays drawn from the upper and lower edges of each riser, as seen in side elevation, will now determine just what parts of the lamp and buttress cast shadows on those risers.

It will sometimes be necessary to find the whole of a shadow on the plane of a step, in order that the part which is real may be accurately found. For example, in the present case it is necessary to find the shadow on the top riser of the whole of the lamp globe, though a preliminary inspection of the figure would have shown that only a part of that shadow is real. The same is true of the shadows of the rings of acanthus leaves on steps L_{3S} M_{3S} and O_{3S} P_{3S}.

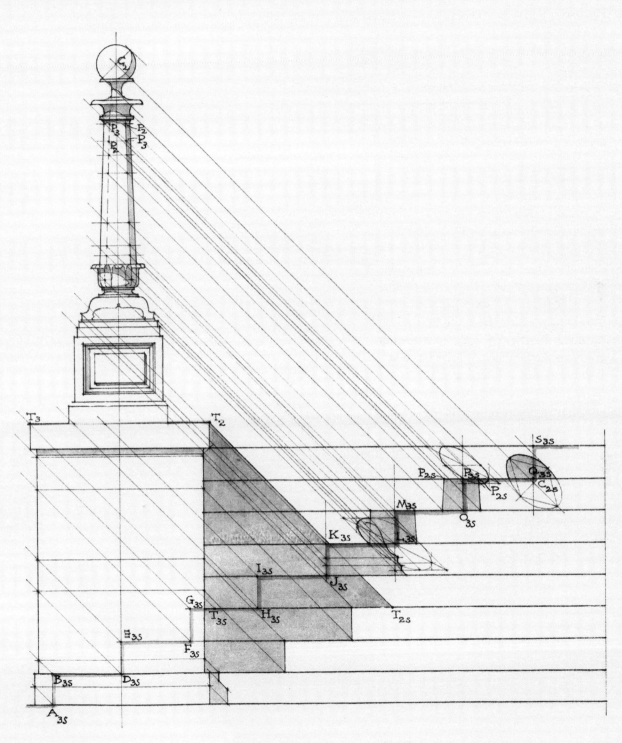

FIGVRE 39

The Shadows of an Arcade
and Its Roof on a Wall Behind It

The determination of the shadows in this case is done by
direct projection, and offers no difficulty.

First find the shadow of the eaves line $C_2 B_2$ on the wall
over the arcade. The shadow of this line is as far below
the line as the line is in front of the wall. (Article VII.)
The depth of the shadow is determined by the forty-five-
degree line $A_2 B_{2S}$.

Next cast the shadows of the ends of the lookouts C_2, D_2,
E_2. Since construction is impracticable at the given scale, we
construct the shadow at a larger scale, as shown in Figure
41, and having thus determined the form of the shadow, we
repeat it at the scale of the elevation, as necessary.

To cast the shadows on the wall, we draw a line $X_3 Y_3$ in
such a position on the elevation that, if $X_3 Y_3$ represents the
face of the wall, then the part of the elevation to the right of
$X_3 Y_3$ will truly represent the side elevation of the portico.
The rest of the construction is so apparent as to need no
detailed explanation.

It has been necessary here to cast a good many
imaginary shadows, such as the shadow of the arch of the
right end of the portico, because it is impossible to tell
from an inspection of such an elevation just what parts will
cast real shadows. We therefore cast the shadows of all parts
except those which evidently cannot be in light. Those
shadows which then prove to be covered by other shadows
are of course imaginary.

In this figure, a good many imaginary shadows have
been drawn, also, merely to render the relation of shadows
to the casting objects more apparent, and to illustrate the
fact that shadows are merely oblique projections of the
objects casting them. (Article XII–1.)

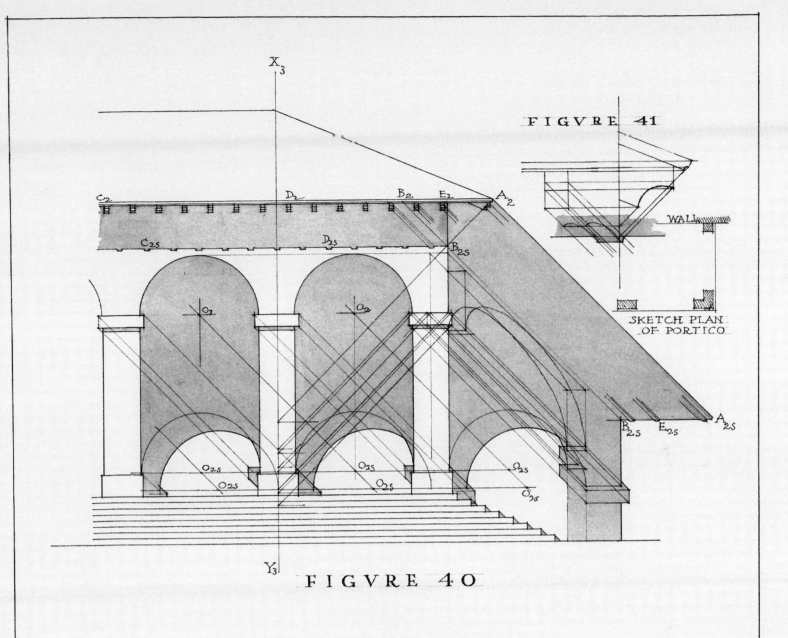

X₃

C₂ D₂ B₂ E₂ A₂

C₂S D₂S B₂S

O₂ O₂

B₂S E₂S A₂S

O₂S O₂S O₂S O₂S O₂S O₂S

Y₃

FIGVRE 40

FIGVRE 41

WALL

SKETCH PLAN
OF PORTICO

The Shades and Shadows on a Roof and Wall of a Circular Tower with a Conical Roof

The determination of these shades and shadows involves only the methods already stated for finding the shades and shadows of circles, cylinders and cones. (Articles XIV, XV, and XVI.) Proceed to determine these singly.

1—*Represent a right side elevation of the tower,* by drawing the profile lines of wall and roof, $X_3 Y_3$, on the front elevation in such position that the left profile line of the tower will serve as the profile in side elevation. Assume in this case that the tower is engaged one-third of its diameter in the wall of the main building.

2—*The shades on the conical roof and on the conical part of the tower near its base.* The shade on the roof cone is found by casting the shadow of the apex A on the plane of the base in plan at A_{1S}, and drawing tangents $A_{1S} B_1$ and $A_{1S} C_1$. The points of tangency B_1 and C_1 are determined with precision by drawing the radii $A_1 B_1$ and $A_1 C_1$ normal to those tangents. B_1 and C_1 are the plans of the feet of the shade lines of the cone. The elevations of these points are B_2 and C_2. Then the shade lines of the cone are $A_2 B_2$ (visible) and $A_2 C_2$ (invisible).

It is evident that from the point W_2, where the shade line passes on to the curved part of the roof, the shade line will run off rapidly toward the right. This part may be drawn from imagination.

The shade line, $Q_2 O_{2S}$, of the conical part of the tower, is found in a similar way.

3—*The shades on the cylindrical parts of the tower.* These are found by drawing on plan the radius $T_1 U_1$ normal to the direction of the tangent rays on plan. In elevation these lines are found at J_{2S}, M_{2S}, N_2 and U_2.

4—*The shadows on the tower of the circular lines whose elevations are* $E_2 F_2$, $G_2 H_2$ *and* $I_2 K_2$, are found by direct projection, using plans and elevations of different points on these lines, drawing rays through these points, and finding where these rays strike the tower. Three or four such shadow points should be sufficient to determine the shadows of each circle on the tower.

[Article XXII continues on page 51]

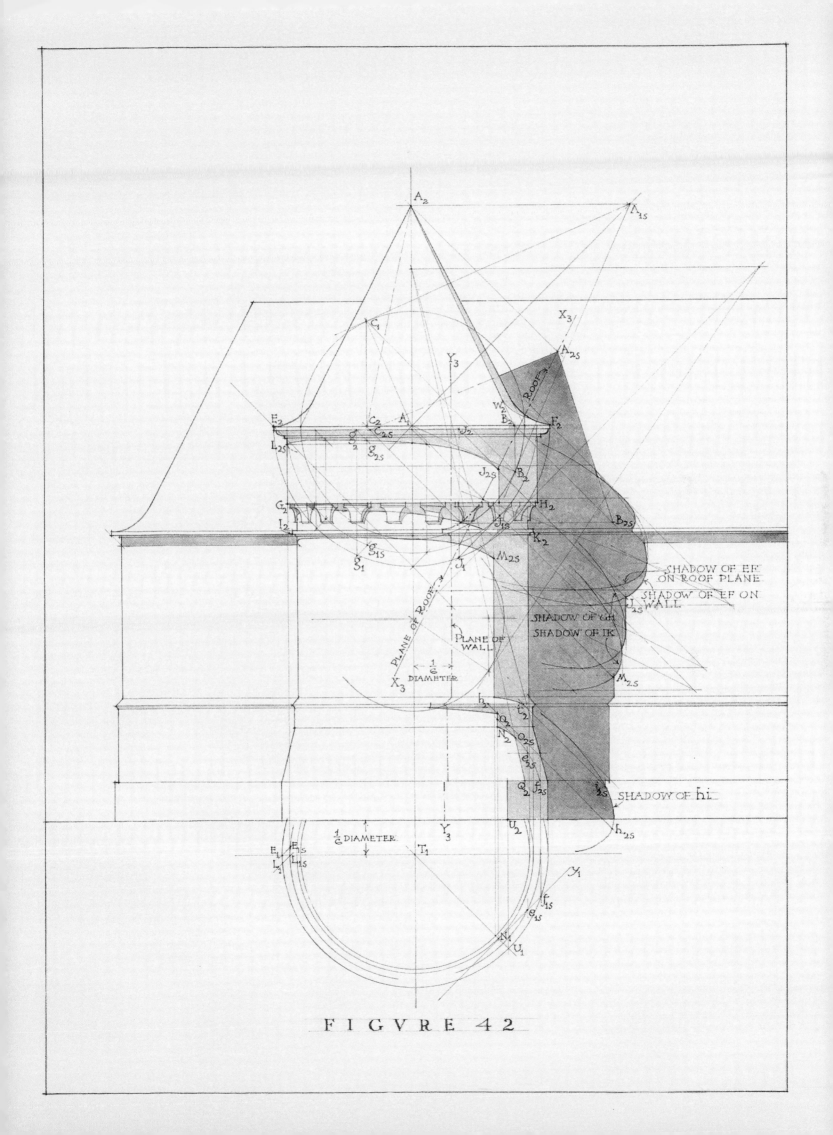

FIGVRE 42

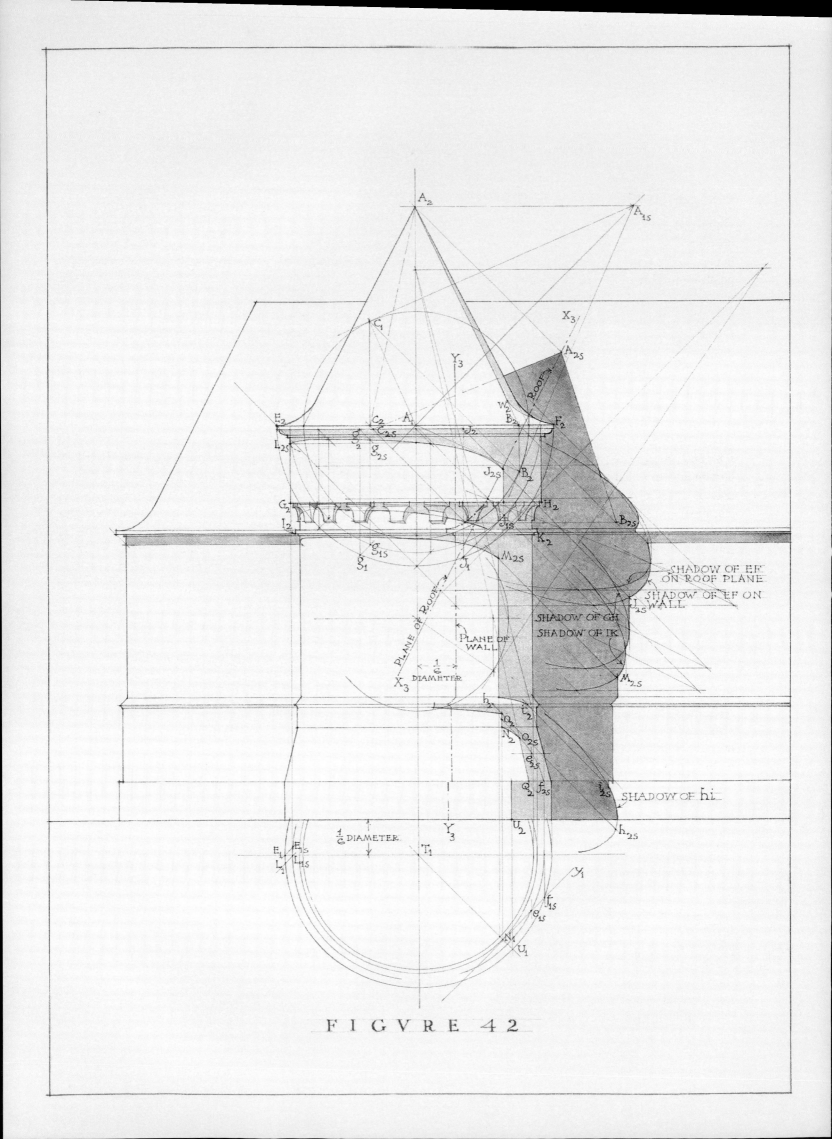

FIGVRE 42

It should be noted that points J_{2S}, M_{2S}, etc., where these shadow lines cross the shade lines of the tower, are found by drawing those rays in plan which are tangent to the tower in plan, and passing back along such rays to the plans of the points of the circles which cast shadows to the shade lines of the tower. Thus by drawing the ray $J_{1S} J_1$ in plan tangent to the plan of the top part of the tower, the point J is determined, which casts its shadow on the shade line of the tower. The elevation of this point is J_2. Then the point where the shadow of the circle crosses the shade line of the tower in elevation is found at J_{2S} by drawing the ray $J_2 J_{2S}$ from J_2 to its intersection with the shade line.

It should also be noted that the profile point L_{2S} of the shadow of EF is *not* the shadow of the point E_2, *and is not found by drawing a forty-five-degree line from* E_2. It will be seen from the plan that the point of the circle EF which does cast its shadow on the profile of the tower at L_{2S} in elevation is on the ray drawn from L_{1S} in plan—that is, at L, the point which in plan is L_1. In this case, L very nearly coincides with E in elevation. Avoid the very common error of determining the profile point of the shadow in such a case by drawing a forty-five-degree line from the profile point of the line casting the shadow.

The point L_{2S} will be at the same level as the point at which the shadow line $L_{2S} J_{2S}$ crosses the axis of the tower. In any surface generated by the revolution of a line about a vertical axis, points on the profile are situated symmetrically with those in front of the axis, with reference to the direction of light. Hence in the case of a symmetrical shadow on such a surface, what is true of points on the axis in elevation is true of points on the profile.

5—*The shadow of the line* $O_2 N_2$ *on the conical part of the tower.* This is the forty-five-degree line $N_1 y_1$ in plan. (Article XIII–3.) By passing from points in the plan of this shadow line to points in its elevation, the line $N_2 O_{2S}$ is determined. Two or three points should be enough to determine the shadow in this and in similar cases, the general form of the curve being known beforehand.

6—*The shadows of the circle* GH *on the corbels below it.* Since the upper parts of the corbels are parts of a cylinder, the shadow may be begun by drawing the shadow of the circle on the cylinder. Since the lower parts of the corbels are double-curved surfaces, it is impracticable to find the shadow on them at a small scale. The student's power of visualization must help him in such instances, or the drawing must be made at a much larger scale and the shadow determined by the slicing method (Article X) or the method of auxiliary shadows (Article IX).

Where the same detail is repeated many times and it is impracticable to construct the shadow accurately at the scale of the drawing in hand, it is often desirable to draw the detail at large scale, and after having determined accurately the form of the shadow at the large scale, to copy it on the smaller drawing.

7—*The shadow of the roof of the tower on the roof of the main building.* Since the shadow of a cone is the shadow of its shade lines, the shadow of the roof of the tower may be cast by casting the shadows of A, B and C and the shadow of the circle EF on the main roof. The shadow of the circle EF is found by casting the shadow of the circumscribing square in which the shadow of the circle may then be inscribed. (Article XIV.)

8—*The shadows of the circle* EF *on the wall of the main building* is found similarly. (Article XIV–2.) Evidently, in this case, there are two circles casting, respectively, parts of the required shadow—the upper and lower edges of the fillet over the gutter moulding. At the scale given, however, the two shadows would so nearly coincide that the shadow of one of the circles may be cast, and that of the other be assumed without appreciable error to be coincident with it.

Shadow of circles GH *and* IK *on the main wall* are to be found as above.

9—*The shadows of the cylindrical parts of the tower,* projected directly on plan, complete the construction.

The Shades and Shadows on a Tuscan Base with the Shadows on a Wall

In this problem the Tuscan base is assumed to stand on a sub-plinth, and to set under a column engaged one-third of its diameter in a wall. The plan of the face of this wall is $X_1 Y_1$; the plan of the center of the column is C_1. The student will readily see the connection between other points and lines of plan and elevation.

First proceed to find the shades and shadows on the column and the base.

1—*The shade line of the drum of the column above the base* is at A_1 in plan, the point at which the plan of a ray is tangent to the plan of the cylinder (Article XVI–3) and at $A_2 B_2$ in elevation.

2—*The shade and shadow on the congé* are found from plan to be at B_2, D_{2S}, E_{2S}.

3—*The shade line on the cincture* at F_2 is found as is that of any upright cylinder.

4—*The shades and shadows on the torus.* There is a shadow on the torus cast by shade lines $F_2 E_{2S}$ and $B_2 A_2$. This so nearly coincides with the profile of the torus that it is impracticable to show it at small scale. The shade on the torus is to be found as follows:

It is evident from an inspection of the plan—

(*a*) That $U_1 V_1$ and $S_1 T_1$ will be axes of symmetry of the shade line in plan.

(*b*) That the lowest point of shadow will lie on $C_1 U_1$ and the highest point on $C_1 V_1$, and that these points will be those at which the true ray R will appear tangent to the profile of the torus when seen in a direction perpendicular to $U_1 V_1$.

(*c*) That two vertical planes of rays tangent to the torus will touch it on its equator at points S_1 and T_1 in plan. (Article XII–10.)

(*d*) That since $U_1 V_1$ is an axis of symmetry of the shade line, if the profile point of the shade line be found, there will also be a point, P_2, of the shade line on the elevation of the axis at the same level.

(*e*) That the points where the shade line crosses the profile of the torus, as seen in front elevation, will be determined by the forty-five-degree tangents to the profile. (To be determined, as always, by drawing the radii of the circles perpendicular to the tangents. Article XII–10.)

To find the highest and lowest points of the shade line proceed as determined above (*b*). Suppose rays tangent to that profile of the torus which is $U_1 V_1$ in plan to have been drawn. Let us now revolve the profile around the axis C_1 until it coincides in plan with $C_1 Z_1$ and in elevation with the front elevation of the torus. Thus the tangent rays will be seen in their true direction with reference to the horizontal plane. Construct the angle r (Figure 44) and draw the tangent $U'_2 G_2$. The point U'_2 is the revolved position of the lowest point of the shade. When the ray $U'_2 G_2$ is revolved back to its true position the point G remains stationary, being in the axis of revolution, and the ray becomes a forty-five-degree line. $U_2 G_2$ is thus the true front elevation of this ray, which contains the point of shade desired. The point U'_2 will evidently move along the level line $U'_2 U_2$. Hence the front elevation of the lowest point of shade is at U_2. The highest point is found in the same way.

To find the points where the shade line is tangent to the profile, draw forty-five-degree tangents to the profile, finding points M_2 and N_2 as determined above (*e*). (Article XII–10.)

The points of shade on the equator are found at S_2 and T_2, as indicated above (*c*).

These points are sufficient to determine the shade line with accuracy, and they may always be easily found.

The student is advised to become so familiar with the form of this shade that he can draw it accurately and quickly from memory without making the construction. He should be able to do this with sufficient accuracy for most rendered drawings at small scale.

Let it be remembered that the shade line is tangent to, and lies wholly within, the apparent profile of the torus. It is a very common fault to draw the inside part of the shade so that if completed it would run off into space and not lie wholly within the profile of the object—as shown in Figure 45.

The shadows of the base, plinth, etc., are now to be found.

5—*Cast the shadow of the top of the drum of the column on the wall*, as explained in Article XIV–2.

6—*Cast the shadow of the shade line of the drum on the wall*, by use of plan, or by merely drawing the ray $A_2 A_{2S}$ from A_2, and the shadow of AB parallel to AB from the point A_{2S} where the ray crosses the shadow line of the circle.

7—*The shadow of the torus on the wall* is most readily found by determining the plans of points L, M, N, P, S, T, U, V, and hence the shadows of these points on the wall by direct projection.

8—The determination of the shadow of the plinth, which needs no explanation, completes the shadow.

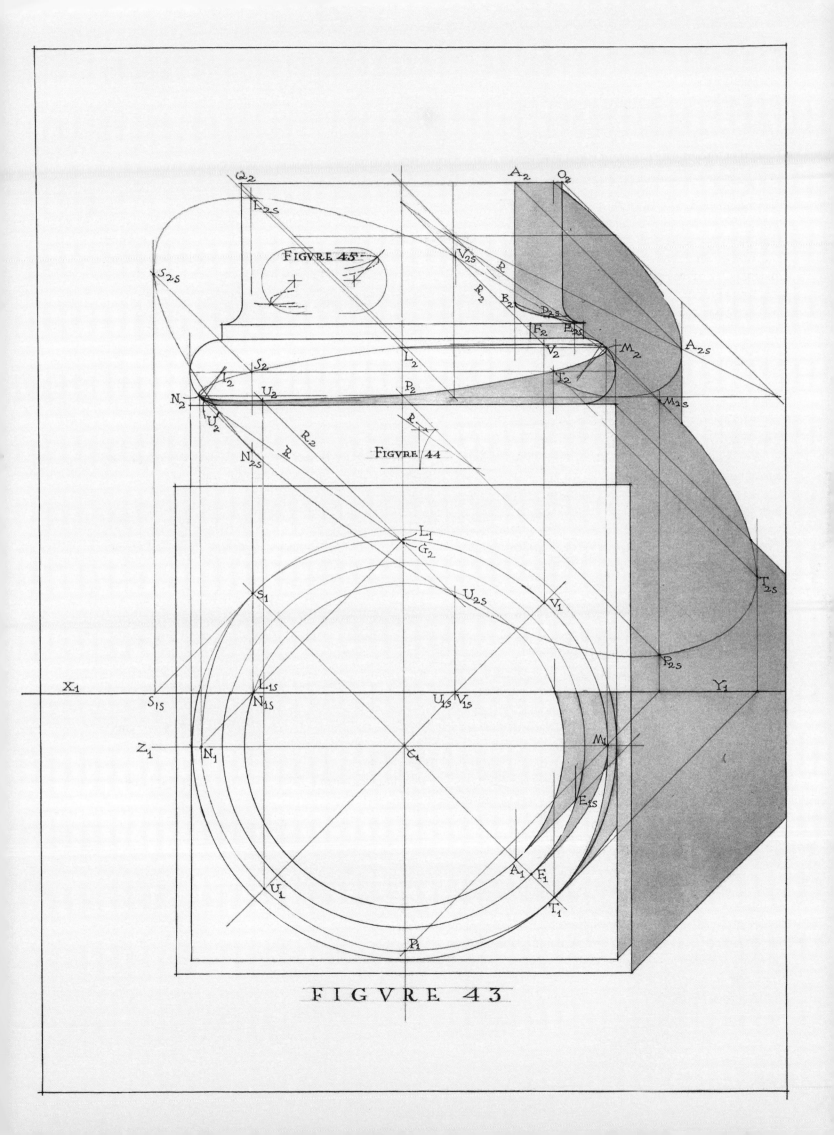

FIGVRE 45

FIGVRE 44

FIGVRE 43

The Shades and Shadows of a Tuscan Capital

The Tuscan capital here shown is that of Vignola. The column is assumed to be engaged one-third of its lower diameter in a wall behind.

First find the shades and shadows on the capital and on the upper part of the column.

1—*The shadow of the fillet on the abacus*, $A_{2S} B_{2S}$. This has a depth equal to the projection of the fillet.

2—*The shade on the ovolo*. The ovolo is the lower portion of a torus, and the shade line $C_{2S} D_{2S} E_2$ is found as in Article XXIII.

3—*The shade line*, $F_2 G_{2S} H_2$, *on the astragal below the neck*, is found in the same way.

4—*The shade line of the column* is found by drawing the radius in plan normal to the direction of the rays.

5—*The shadow of the left lower edge of the abacus*, K_2, *on the capital and column*. Being a line perpendicular to the front plane, its shadow is the forty-five-degree line $K_2 K_{2S}$.

6—*The shadow of the front lower edge of the abacus*, $K_2 J_2$, *on the neck of the column*. This is a circle whose radius is equal to the radius of the neck of the column, $Q_2 K_{2S}$, and whose center is Q_2, in the axis at the distance $P_2 Q_2$ below the line $K_2 J_2$, equal to the distance of that line in front of the axis. (Article XVI-4.)

7—*The shadow* $U_{2S} V_{2S}$ *of the same line on the cincture* $W_2 X_2$ is found in the same way.

8—*The shadow of the part* $C_2 D_2$ *of the same line on the ovolo*. Find the oval curve $y_2 z_2 a_2$ of the ovolo; that is, its shadow on the oblique vertical plane whose plan is $O_1 b_1$. (Article XIV-4.) Find the shadow $J_2 Q_2$ of JK on the same plane. (Article XIII-4.) Then a_2 and z_2 are the shadows of the two points where the shadow of KJ crosses the shade line of the torus. (Article IX-b.) We then pass back along rays through these points to find points C_{2S} and D_{2S} on the torus. The highest point of the shadow will evidently be at e_{2S}. The point f_{2S} is on the same level as C_{2S} and symmetrically situated with reference to the axis.

9—*The shadow of the part of the shade line whose elevation is* $D_{2S} g_2$ *on the cincture* $X_2 W_2$ is found by the use of the plan of the shade line of the torus. The point g_{2S} where it leaves the cincture is readily found by passing back along the ray from the point of intersection h_2 of the auxiliary shadows of the ovolo (Section 19, below) and of the circle $W_2 X_2$ on the auxiliary oblique plane $O_1 b_1$. (Article IX.) *[Article XXIV continues on page 57]*

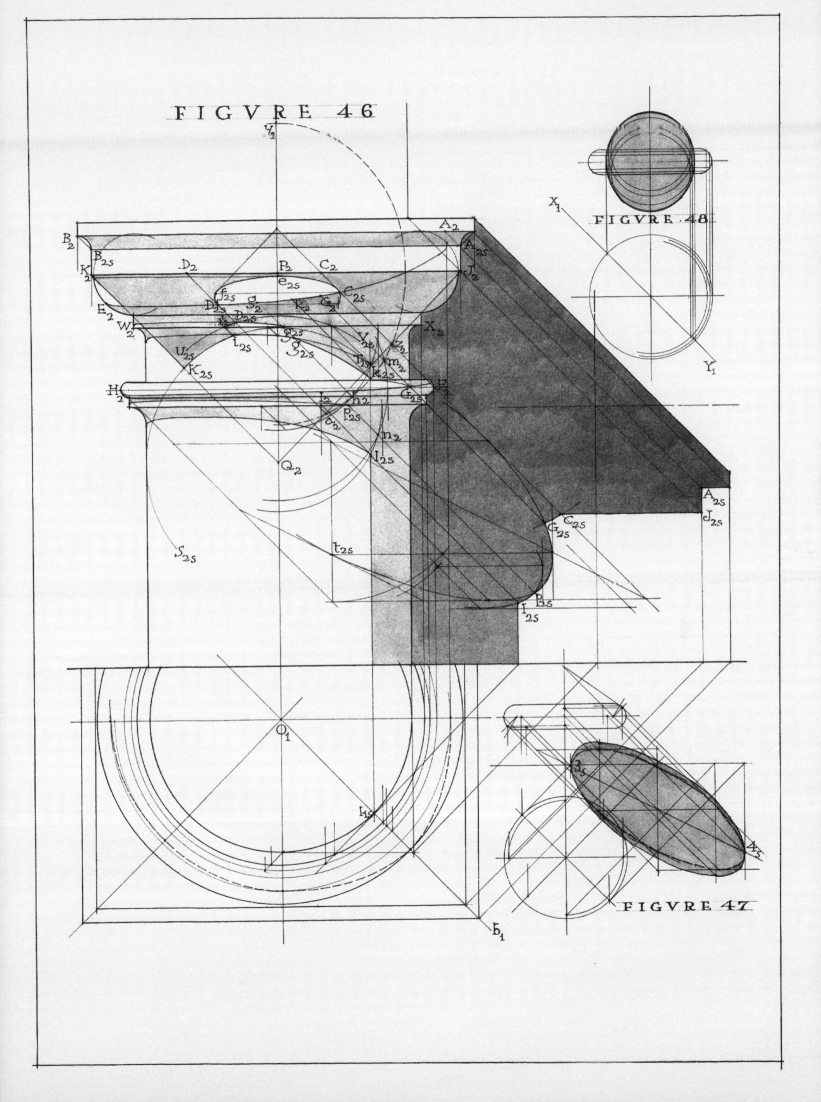

F I G V R E 4 6

F I G V R E 48

F I G V R E 47

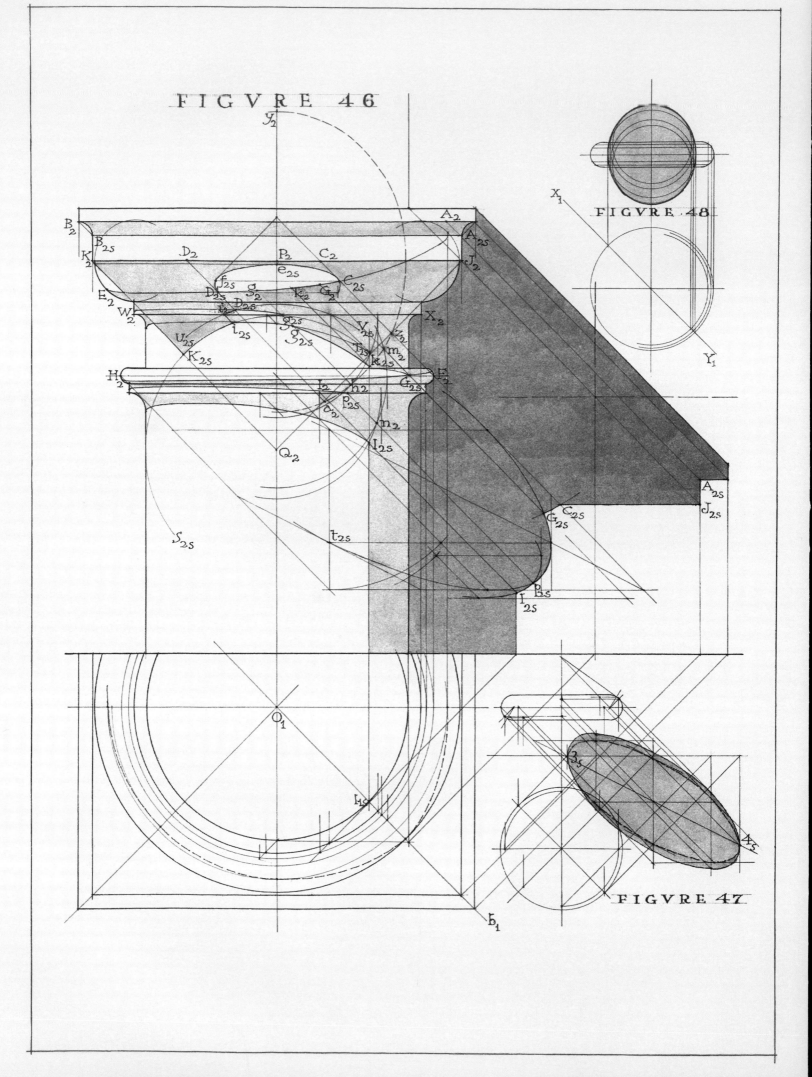

FIGVRE 46

FIGVRE 48

FIGVRE 47

10—*The shadow* i_{2S} g_{2S} *of the circle* W_2 X_2 *on the neck of the column* is found by the use of the plan; or, the two points i_{2S} and g_{2S} having been already determined, this shadow may readily be drawn without the finding of other points.

11—*The shadow* g_{2S} k_{2S} *of the ovolo on the neck of the column* may be drawn from imagination with sufficient accuracy after k_{2S} has been found. The intersection of the oval curve y_2 z_2 a_2 with the shade line I_{2S} k_{2S} evidently determines k_{2S} exactly. (Article IX.)

12—*The shadow* G_{2S} *of the point* G_2 is found by passing back along the ray from the intersection of the oval curve of the ovolo and that of the astragal at m_2. (Article IX.)

13—*The shadow of the astragal* H_2 F_2 *on the cincture below it* may be found by use of the plan, or by the slicing method; or, point P_{2S} may be exactly determined by passing back along the ray from the intersection, n_2, of the shadows of HF and of the lower circle of the cincture on the oblique plane whose plan is O_1 b_1 (Article IX), and the shadow may then be drawn from imagination.

14—*The shadow of this cincture on the column* is found by the use of the plan.

Now proceed to cast the shadow of the capital and column on the wall.

15—*The shadow* G_{2S} p_{2S} I_{2S} is cast by the astragal, and is determined by merely casting on the wall the shadow of the equator circle of the astragal, which nearly enough coincides with its actual shadow. (Figure 47.) I_{2S} p_{2S} is the shadow of the lower edge of the cincture below H_2 F_2. This shadow may be omitted in drawings at small scale.

16—*The shadow of points* C_{2S} *and* G_2 may be found by drawing the rays through C_2 and G_2 until they intersect the shadows of C_2 J_2 and H_2 F_2.

17—The casting of the other shadows on the wall needs no explanation.

These shadows have been explained fully in detail since they furnish a good example of an analysis which is somewhat complicated because it involves a number of processes, none of which, however, present any difficulty when considered singly.

It should be noted that the use of the method of auxiliary shadows (Article IX) has been very convenient in this case; the auxiliary shadows being cast on the vertical auxiliary plane passing through the axis of the column, backward to the left at the angle of forty-five degrees. Similar preliminary constructions have been explained in Article XIII–4, and Article XIV–4.

These shadows might have been determined also by the slicing method. This would have been no less laborious, however, and not nearly so accurate, though it would have been simpler in analysis, since it would have involved but one process.

18—Figure 47 shows the construction of the actual shadow on a front plane of the torus there shown, and that of the equatorial circle of the torus, the latter being the dotted inner line. Evidently, the two curves will coincide only at 3_s and 4_s—the shadows of the points where the shade line of the torus crosses the equatorial circle.

From this construction it is plain that the shadows on front planes of such flat tori as usually occur in architectural work may be found accurately enough for drawings at a small scale by casting the shadow of the equatorial circles of the tori.

19—Figure 48 shows the construction of the shadow of a torus on a vertical plane passing back to the left through its axis, making the angle forty-five degrees with the front plane. This shadow is, of course, the envelope of the shadows on the oblique plane of the circles of the torus. (Article IX and Article XIV–4.) This shadow will be called the oval curve of the torus. The student should be familiar with it, as it is often very useful in finding exactly particular points of shadow in problems to follow, as it was in the preceding problem.

The Shades and Shadows
of an Urn and Plinth

The urn and plinth shown in Figure 49 are supposed to be placed in front of a wall parallel to a front plane, the axis of the urn being at a distance x from the wall.

The shades and shadows on the urn should be found first.

1—*The cincture AB* is part of a cylinder whose shade line is found from plan at C_2 in elevation.

2—*The quarter-round moulding* $D_2 E_2$ below it may be regarded as part of a torus whose shade line $F_2 G_2$ is found as shown in Article XXIII.

3—*The shadow of the edge DE* on the body of the urn may be found by the slicing method. The plans of the slicing planes are shown at $1_1, 2_1, 3_1, 4_1$, etc., and the elevations of the slices cut by those planes on the surface of the urn are at $1_2, 2_2, 3_2$, etc. From these are determined the shadow points $1_S, 2_S, 4_S$, etc.

4—The shade line $H_{2S} 8_{2S}$ may be assumed with reasonable accuracy to be that on a cylinder, $H_{2S} 8_{2S}$ being drawn nearly parallel to the right profile of the urn from point 8_{2S}. 8_{2S} is determined by the forty-five-degree tangent to the plan of the horizontal circle through 8_{2S}.

5—*The part of the urn* $Z_2 Z_2 I_2 J_2$ is part of a torus, and its shade line $K_2 L_2$ may be found as in Article XXIII, or by the slicing method. The latter may be conveniently used here, as it will also be used in finding shadow $M_{2S} N_{2S}$ and $O_{2S} P_{2S} Q_{2S}$.

The shadow on the torus $b_2 c_2$. Assume on the urn, a little below L_2, an auxiliary circle. Evidently, the shadow of this circle will very nearly coincide with the shadow of that part of $L_2 K_2$ which would fall on the torus below. Cast the shadow of this circle on the forty-five-degree auxiliary plane. (Article XIV–4.) Cast the shadow of the equator circle of the torus $b_2 c_2$ on the same plane. From the intersection of these two auxiliary shadows, draw the elevation of a ray, producing it until it intersects the shade line of the torus $b_2 c_2$ at N_{2S}. This point will evidently be the point where the shadow of the line $L_2 K_2$ crosses the shade line of torus $b_2 c_2$.

6—*Shadow line of torus* $b_2 c_2$ on the cincture below it is found from the slices. The point at the right where it leaves the cincture may be found as in section 5, above, or by passing back to the lower edge of the cincture along the ray from the intersection of the shadows on the wall of that edge of the cincture and of the torus. In the latter case the shadows on the wall would serve as auxiliary shadows.

7—*The shade line on the cincture below the upper scotia* and those on the two cinctures below the lower scotia are found as above in section 1.

8—*The shades on the two tori* $d_2 e_2$ *are drawn from imagination*, as is the shadow of the upper torus on the lower. The two may of course be drawn at larger scale and these lines determined exactly. The shadow of the lower torus de on the cincture below it may be found exactly at larger scale. At the scale here given it would be practical to find the point g_{2S}, where the shadow of the torus leaves the cincture, by the method of auxiliary shadows as in section 5, and to then draw the shadow from imagination.

9—*The shadows of the cinctures on the scotias below them* are found by the slicing method.

The shadows of the urn on the wall may now be determined, as follows:

10—*Shadow* $h_{2S} F_{2S} G_{2S}$ is the shadow of the shade line $G_2 F_2 h_2$ of the torus DE. *Shadow* $E_{2S} G_{2S} 8_{2S}$ is that of circle DE. *Shadow* $m_{2S} H_{2S} n_{2S}$ is that of circle lm. *Shadow* $p_{2S} q_{2S}$ is that of circle $L_2 p_2$. *Shadow* $s_{2S} u_{2S} t_{2S}$ is that of the cincture $s_2 t_2$. Shadows on the wall of other horizontal circles of the urn will be found to lie within the above lines, and hence are imaginary.

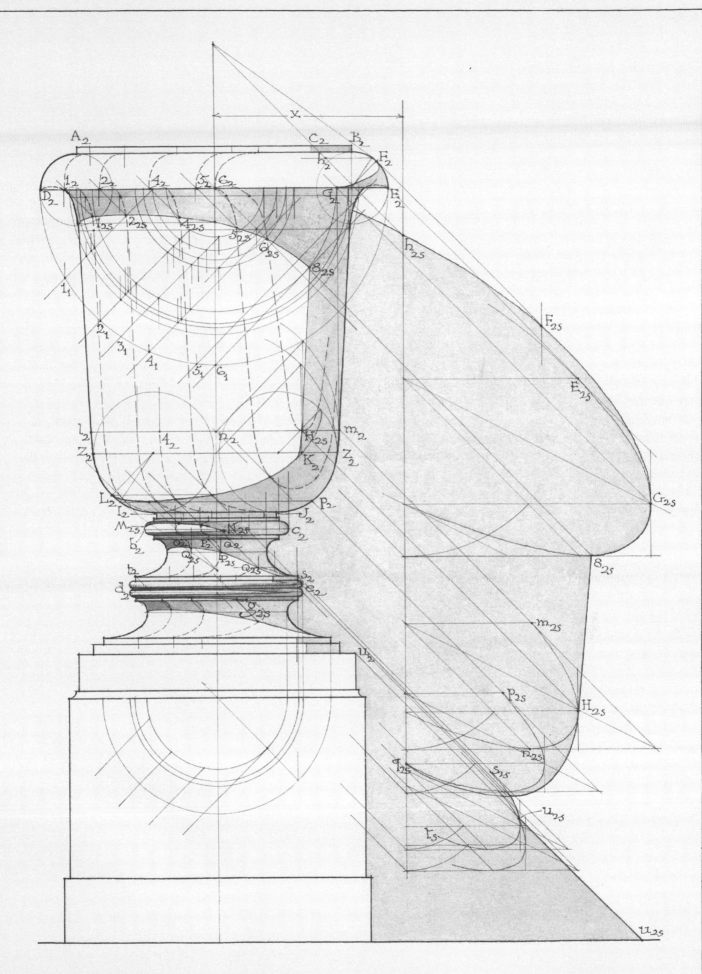

FIGVRE 49

The Shades and Shadows on a Baluster

1—*The shadow of the edges of the abacus* on the echinus and the cincture below it are found as in the case of the Tuscan capital. (Article XXIV.)

2—*The shade on the echinus* is determined in the same way as is that on the ovolo. (Article XXIV.)

3—*The shadow of the echinus* on the cincture below it is found by determining points of the plan of the shade line of the echinus, and then finding points of the required shadow by direct projection. Axial point B_{2S} and profile point C_{2S} are on the same level.

4—*The shadow of the lower edge of the cincture* on the baluster is found by the method of auxiliary shadows. Shadows of the circle of the lower edge of the cincture and of circles g_2, h_2, etc., are cast on the oblique plane (Article XIV–4), and points of the required shadow of the circle of the cincture on circles g_2 h_2, etc., may be obtained by passing back along rays through points of intersection of the auxiliary shadows. The slicing method might have been used for this shadow, as also for that of the scotia below.

5—*The shade on the middle part of the baluster* is that on a cone whose apex is at A and whose profile lines on front elevation are $A_2\, F_2$ and $A_2\, G_2$.

6—*Shade line* $H_2\, I_2$ is that on the lower part of the torus $F_2\, G_2\, K_2\, L_2$.

7—*Shadow lines of this torus* on the cincture below it and of the edge of the cincture on the scotia below it are found by the method of auxiliary shadows as in section 3 above.

8—*The shade on the cincture below the scotia* is that on a cylinder.

9—*The shade on the moulding below the cincture* is found as in the case of the circular torus.

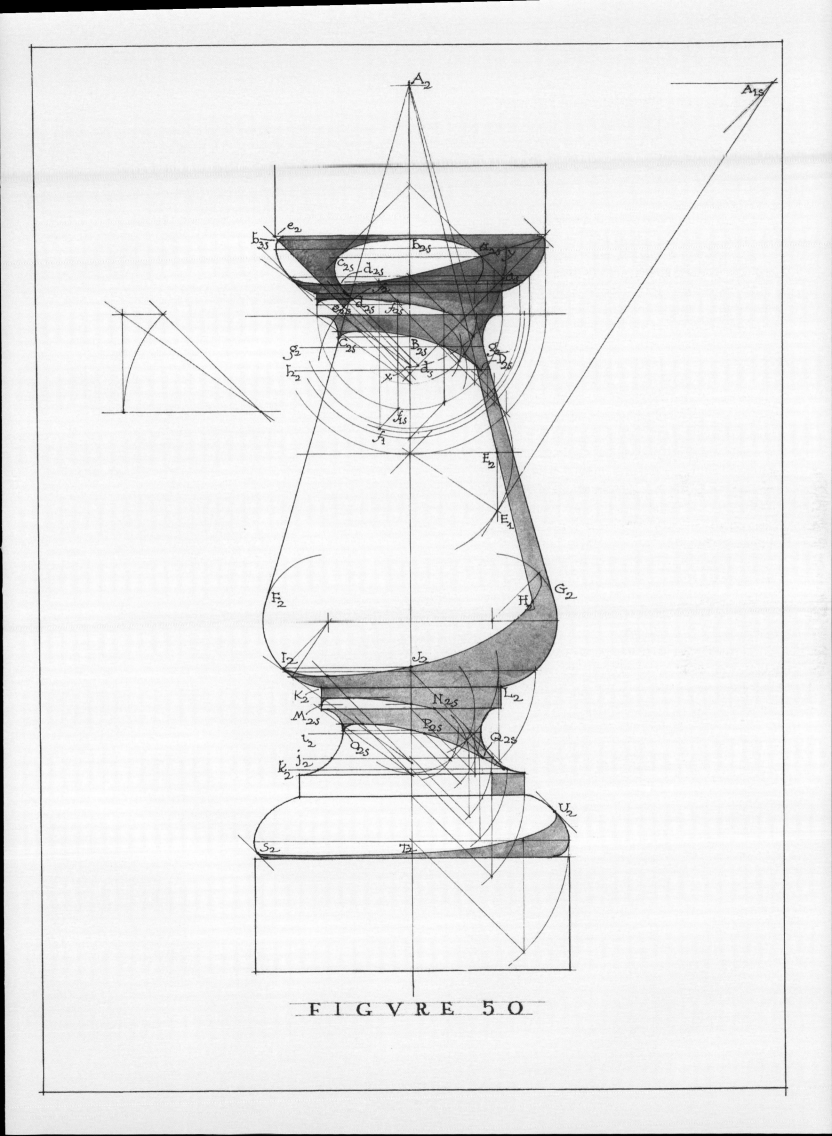

FIGVRE 50

The Shades and Shadows of a Cornice over a Door Head, with Consoles and Modillions, Etc.

1—*The shades and shadows on the mouldings of the cornice* are readily found by direct projection.

2—*The shades and shadows on the modillions and on the console* are found by direct projection and from imagination, using the section and side elevation $X_3 Y_3$.

3—*The shadows of the modillions and of the console on the wall* are found by direct projection. In the case of the modillions, cast first the shadows of the two rectangles containing the scrolls of the right and left faces of a modillion, as E F. Next, cast the shadow of the modillion band. Then cast the shadows of the rectangles containing the forward scrolls on the right and left faces of the modillion. Next, cast the shadow of the forward tip of the rib of the leaf under the scrolls. The shadows of the scrolls of the right and left faces of the modillions may then be drawn within the shadows of these circumscribing rectangles, and the rib of the leaf may be sketched in place and the leaf drawn around it from imagination. This gives a shadow of the form $E_{2S} F_{2S}$.

The shadows of the scrolls of the right face of the console are found in the same way, by using the auxiliary shadows of the rectangle circumscribing those scrolls. The left face of the lower scroll also casts a shadow which is similarly found. Points of the shadow of the part of the right edge GH of the console are found by direct projection.

The shadows of modillions on drawings at such scales as those of drawings ordinarily rendered in practice may be simplified to the form shown at $I_{2S} J_{2S}$ with good effect.

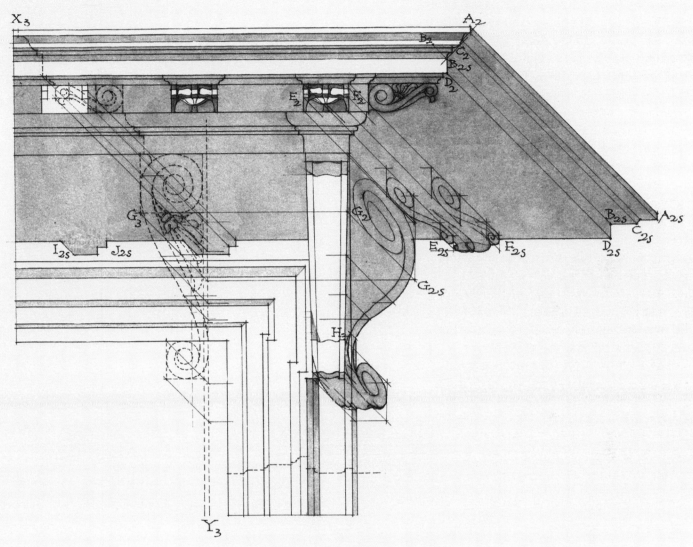

X_3
A_2
B_2
C_2
B_{2S}
D_2
F_2 F_2
G_3
G_3
I_{2S} J_{2S}
G_2
B_{2S} A_{2S}
E_{2S} F_{2S} C_{2S}
D_{2S}
G_{2S}
H_2
Y_3

FIGVRE 51

The Shades and Shadows on a Circular Building with a Domical Roof, Seen in Section

1—*The shadow, B_2 A_{2S} C_{2S}, of* BAC *on the inner surface of the wall and dome* is the shadow on a circular niche. (Article XVII.) The breaks in this shadow at D_{2S} E_{2S} and F_{2S} may be found by determining parts of the shadow of BAC on these fascias.

2—*The shadow of* G_{2S} H_2, *on the face of the cornice*, G_{2S} H_{2S}, is found in the same way, by the use of the plans of the cornice and of the line C_2 I_2. It is to be noted that the true intersection of the window jam and the dome is not the part of the circle of the dome, as here shown for convenience, but is actually the dotted line in elevation, H_2 I_2.

3—*The shadows of the interior cornices* on the cylindrical part of the wall are found by direct projection, plans being used.

4—*The shadow, H_{2S} I_{2S}, of* HI is found by direct projection, plans being used.

5—*The shadows of the profiles of the mouldings at* K *and* L may be assumed to be equal and parallel to these profiles, since the latter are practically parallel to the part of the cylindrical wall on which they fall.

6—*The shadows in the barrel-vaulted heads of the windows* are to be found with the help of their side elevations (the line Q_3 P_3 Q_{3S} being here used as such side elevations). (Article XVI–6.)

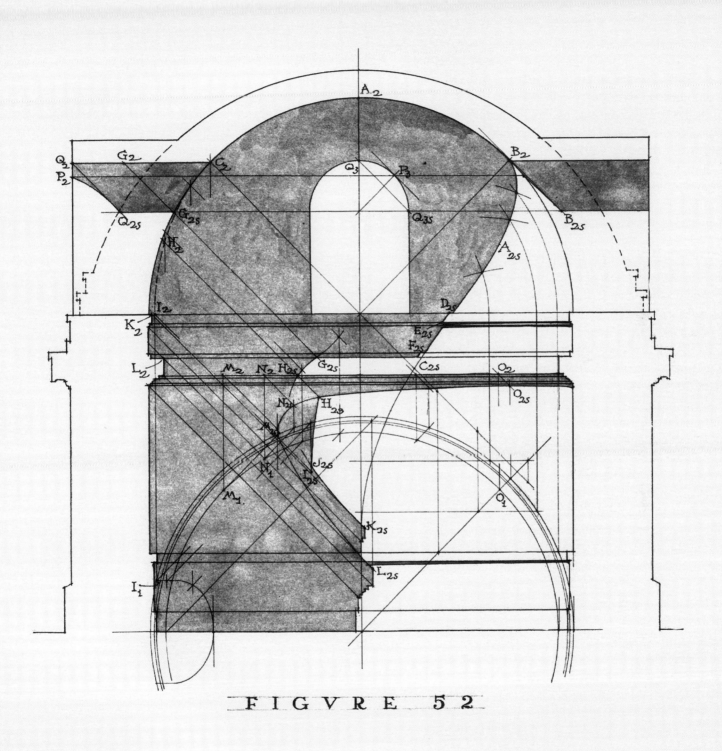

The Shades and Shadows on a Pediment

The method here shown for finding the shadows on the raking mouldings of the pediment, and the shadows of those mouldings on the tympanum, is a variation of the slicing method. (Article X.)

Figure 53 shows a sketch plan of the pediment, d_1 being the plan of the fillet over the crown-moulding, g_1 the face of the frieze, etc.

It is evident that the distance, such as $b_1 c_1$, of any point or line of the pediment from the wall can be readily obtained from a right section of the raking mouldings; that the forty-five-degree slicing plane whose plan is $x_1 y_1$ will cut a vertical line on the plane of the frieze; that the distance in elevation, as $b_1 c_1$, of any point, as b, of this forty-five-degree slice from the vertical line on the frieze will be the same as $a_1 c_1$, the distance of that point from the face of frieze.

Hence, to construct the forty-five-degree vertical slices on the right and left slopes of the pediment shown in Figure 54, proceed as follows: Suppose that the profile $A_2 B_2$ is also that of the right section of the raking parts of the pediment, this being nearly enough true in drawings at small scale. Draw on the right and left slopes of the pediment vertical lines at any convenient place to represent the lines of the slices on the face of the frieze or tympanum. To the left of these lines lay off with a measuring strip the distances 1, 2, 3, 4, etc., equal to distances 1, 2, 3, 4, etc., of corresponding points from the face of the tympanum, these distances being gotten from the profile at A_2. From the points thus determined, the forty-five-degree slices are drawn. The shade and shadow points in these slices are then readily found. Since most of the shade and shadow lines are parallel to the raking lines of the pediment, a single point will determine them, and it will be necessary to construct only one slice for each slope of the pediment.

The application of this method is more clearly shown in Figure 55, which is a detail at larger scale of the middle part of the two uppermost mouldings of the pediment shown in Figure 54.

The shadow of point B will be at B_{2S}, the point where the elevation of the ray through B_2 intersects the shadow line of BG.

The straight part, $A_{2S} C_{2S}$, of the shadow of AC evidently ends at the miter line, $B_2 Z_2$, of the crown-moulding.

The shadow of $C_2 B_2$ on the crown-moulding may be found by the method of auxiliary shadows (Article IX), as follows: Suppose an auxiliary front plane to cut through the crown-moulding. It will cut on it lines parallel to the raking lines of the moulding. Suppose the raking line whose right-hand part passes through D_{2S} to have been cut by such a plane. Then an examination of the forty-five-degree section on the left will show that the auxiliary plane cuts on the forty-five-degree section plane the vertical line $X_2 Y_2$, and that the shadow of the line $A_2 B_2$ on the auxiliary plane is the dotted line $F_{2S} D_{2S}$. Now the raking line through D_{2S} is in the auxiliary plane and also in the crown-moulding. Then the point D_{2S} where this line intersects the auxiliary shadow line $F_{2S} D_{2S}$ is a point of the shadow of $C_2 B_2$ on the moulding.

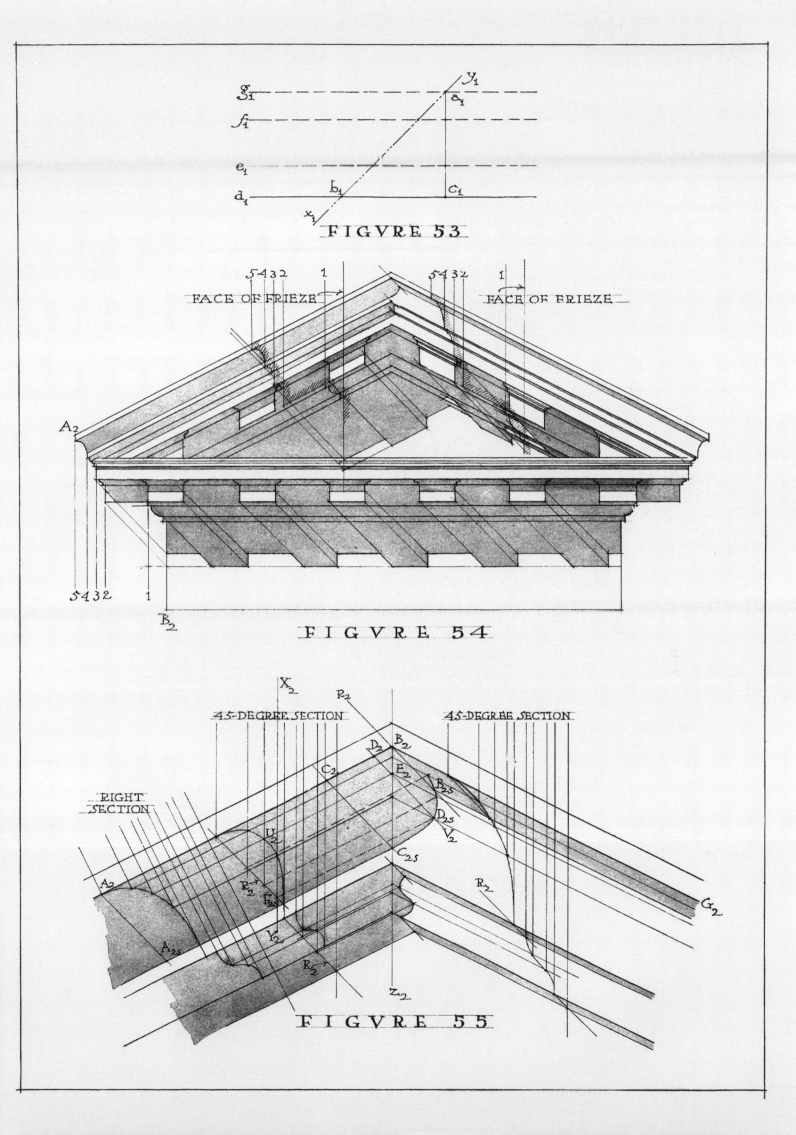

$$g_1 \qquad\qquad\qquad\qquad\qquad\qquad a_1 \quad y_1$$

$$f_1$$

$$e_1$$

$$d_1 \qquad\qquad\qquad b_1 \qquad\qquad\qquad c_1$$

$$x_1$$

FIGVRE 53

5 4 3 2   1   5 4 3 2   1

FACE OF FRIEZE   FACE OF FRIEZE

A_2

5 4 3 2   1

B_2

FIGVRE 54

X_2 R_2

45-DEGREE SECTION   45-DEGREE SECTION

D_2 B_2

C_2 E_2 B_{2S}

RIGHT
SECTION D_{2S}

U_2 V_2

C_{2S}

A_2 R_2 R_2 G_2

F_{2S}

A_{2S} V_2

R_2

Z_2

FIGVRE 55

The Shades and Shadows
of a Greek Doric Capital

The example shown in Figure 56 is taken from the Parthenon. The nature of the shadows here shown was determined from a drawing at larger scale than that of the figure, and the results were copied in Figure 56 in parts where the scale of that figure did not permit accurate construction.

1—*The shadow of the left edge of the abacus* is the forty-five-degree line $A_2 A_{2S}$. (Article XIII–1.)

2—*The shadow, $A_{2S} C_{2S} D_{2S}$, of the front edge of the abacus* on the neck of the column is found by direct projection.

3—*The shadow of the front edge of the abacus on the echinus* is found by constructing the plan, $J_{1S} K_{1S} L_{1S} M_{1S}$, of this shadow from its side elevation, and constructing its front elevation, $J_{2S} K_{2S} L_{2S} M_{2S}$, etc., from plan.

4—*The shade on the echinus* is determined by assuming the echinus as coincident with the cone whose apex is O. The shade line of this cone is $O_2 I_2$ in elevation.

5—*Other details* of the shadow present no difficulty. The shadow $F_{2S} G_{2S}$ is cast by the shade line of the echinus.

Figure 57 shows the shadow of this capital on a wall behind it. The dotted lines show the shadows of the edges of imaginary lintels.

FIGVRE 56

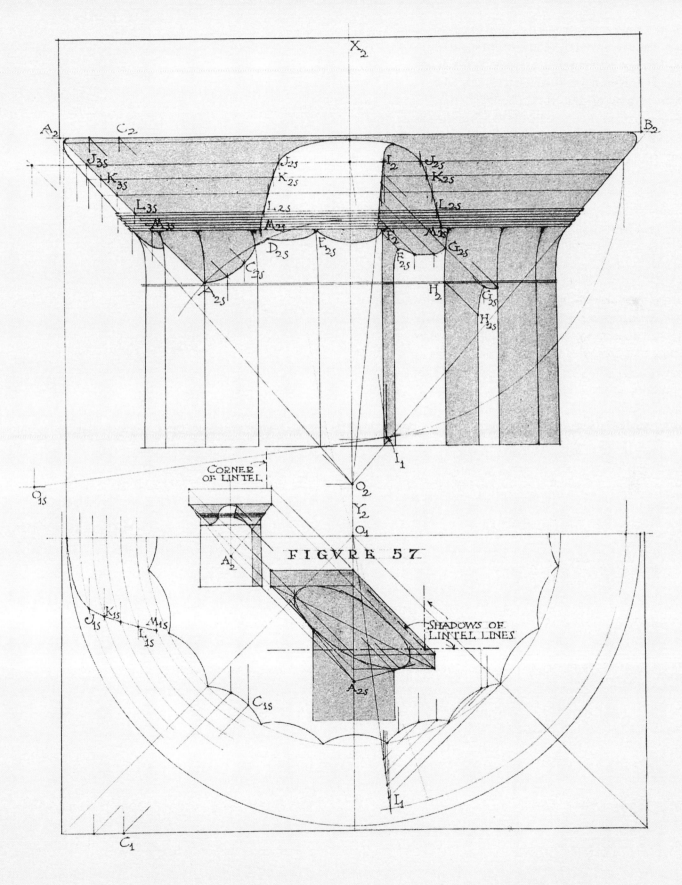

CORNER
OF LINTEL

FIGVRE 57

SHADOWS OF
LINTEL LINES

Article XXXI. FIGURES 58 AND 59.

The Shades and Shadows
of the Roman Tuscan Order

In Figure 58 the column is assumed to be engaged one-third
of its lower diameter in a wall behind it.

Since it will be convenient in this case to use the side
elevation of the order, rather than the plan, in connection
with the front elevation, draw line $X_3 Y_3$ on the front
elevation, one-sixth of the diameter to the left of the axis
of the column. If then the line $X_3 Y_3$ be taken to represent
the face of the wall in side elevation, the part of the figure
to the right of that line will represent the side elevation
of the order.

Then proceed to cast the shades and shadows in
accordance with principles which have been explained
in detail heretofore. Determine the shades and shadows
on the various parts of the order before casting the shadows
of those parts. The draftsman should become quite as
familiar with these shadows and with those of the orders to
follow as with the orders themselves, and should be able
to draw from memory those which it is impracticable to cast
at small scales, such as those on the capital and base.

The shadows on the wall in the case of Figure 58 are
supposed to fall on a wall unbroken by mouldings, etc.

Figure 59 shows the shadow of a detached column
on a wall behind it, the lines of imaginary lintels that might
be placed on the column being shown by dotted lines.

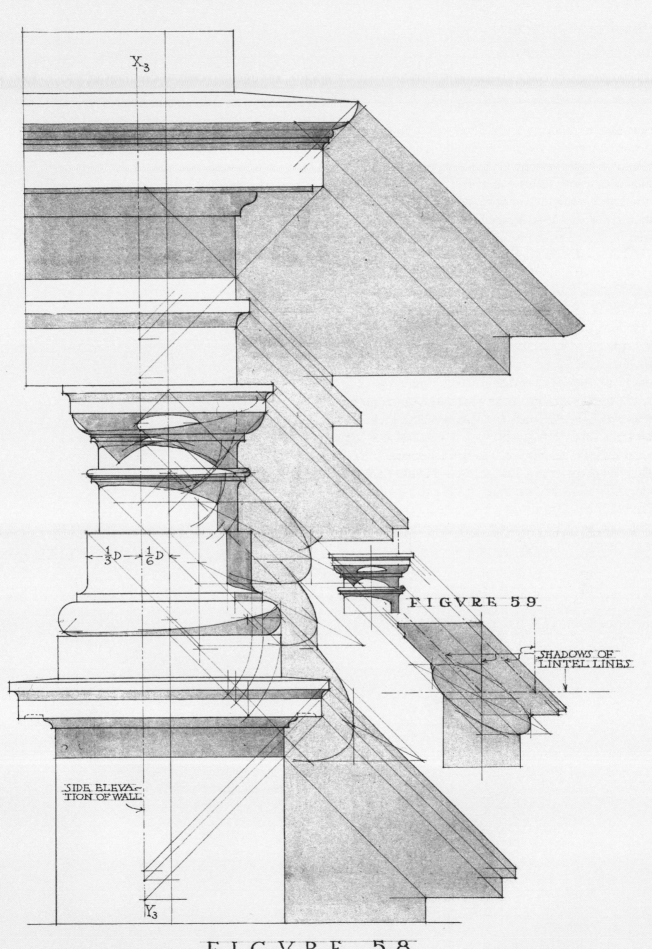

X₃

⅓D ⅙D

SIDE ELEVA-
TION OF WALL

Y₃

FIGVRE 59

SHADOWS OF
LINTEL LINES

FIGVRE 58

The Shades and Shadows
of the Roman Doric Order

Figure 60 shows the shades and shadows of the Roman mutular Doric order of Vignola, the column being engaged, as in the preceding example, in an unbroken wall one-sixth of a diameter back of the axis of the column.

No new principles or details are involved, and the student will have no difficulty in analyzing the construction shown.

Figures 61 and 63 show shadows of various details drawn at enlarged scales, and Figure 62 shows those of an unengaged column, the shadows of imaginary lintel lines being dotted in.

Note that the shadow on the wall of the order with the profiles as here shown, is made up almost wholly of horizontal, perpendicular, and forty-five-degree lines, when drawn at the scale of Figure 60, or smaller. The curves of the crown-moulding and of the other curved mouldings, being practically all in shade or shadow, do not cast real shadows.

At small scale, the shadow of the left lower edge of the mutules may be drawn as a single forty-five-degree line, without the breaks shown in Figure 60. The guttae under the taenia are actually parts of cones, but may, at small scale, be considered as cylindrical.

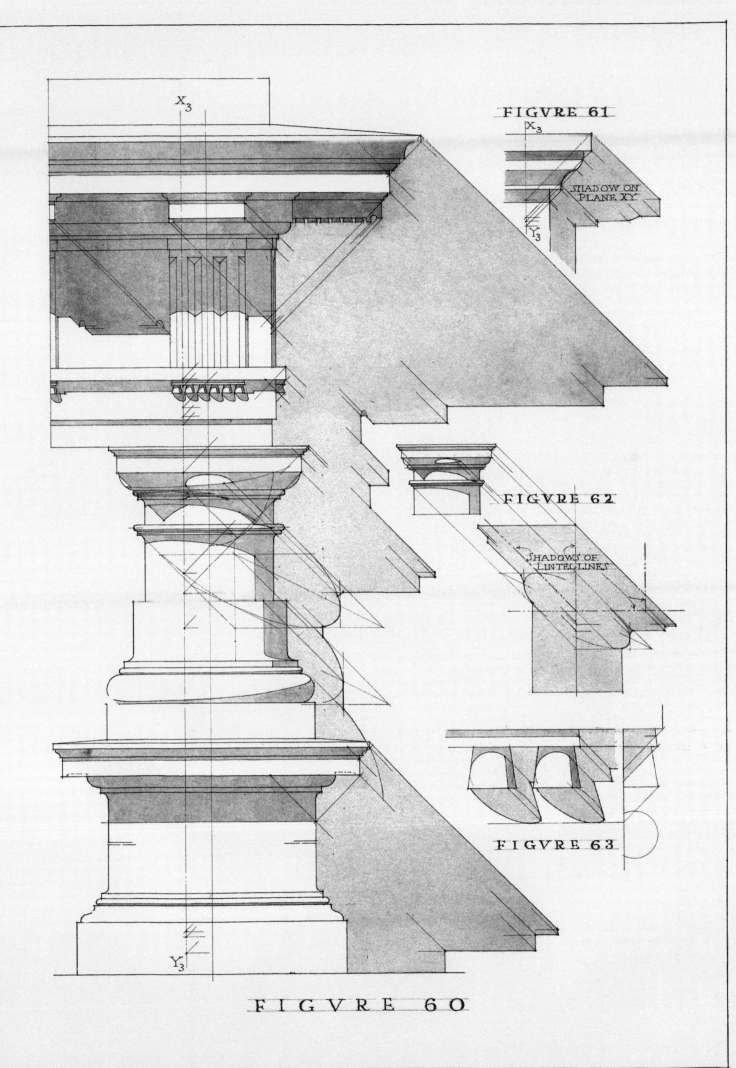

FIGVRE 61

X₃

SHADOW ON
PLANE XY

Y₃

FIGVRE 62

SHADOWS OF
LINTEL LINES

FIGVRE 63

FIGVRE 60

The Shades and Shadows
of the Roman Ionic Order

Figure 64 shows the Roman Ionic order according
to Vignola, with its shades and shadows. The column is
engaged one-third of its lower diameter in the wall behind,
as in the preceding examples.

In this case are also shown the shadows on the
entablature of a section of the entablature returning toward
the front, whose profile is $A_2 B_2 F_2 C_2$; the length of the
return at A is assumed to be x (shown in plan, Figure 65,
as the length x). If now we draw the vertical line $Y_2 Z_2$
at the distance x from the fillet of the crown-moulding A_2,
$Y_2 Z_2$ may be truly considered the side elevation of the
section which is $A_2 B_2 F_2 C_2$ in front elevation, and
$A_2 B_2 F_2 C_2$ will then truly represent, with reference to $Y_2 Z_2$,
the side elevation of the entablature over the column facing
the front. The construction of the shadow of the section line
then becomes easy. Suppose it be required to cast the
shadow of any point of it, as B. The side elevation of B is
B_3. Its shadow on the entablature in side elevation is,
then, at B_{3S}. Then in front elevation the shadow will be on
the horizontal line through B_{3S}, and also on the front
elevation of the ray through B_2; hence B_{2S} is at the
intersection of these two lines.

Suppose it be desired to find what point of the section
line casts its shadow on a certain line of the entablature,
as, for example, the upper edge of the taenia CE. The side
elevation of CE is the point C_2. The side elevation of
the ray which cast shadow at this level is $C_2 F_3$. Then F_3
is the side elevation of the point of the section line
which casts its shadow on the edge CE of the taenia.
The front elevation of F is F_2, and the front elevation of
the ray through F is $F_2 F_{2S}$. The front elevation of the edge
of the taenia is $C_2 E_2$. Hence F_{2S} is the shadow of F.

Thus it is easy to determine just what points of the
section line ABFC cast shadow on given parts of the
entablature facing the front.

The line $S_3 T_3$, representing the side elevation
of the face of the wall in which the column is engaged, is
placed, as in preceding examples, one-sixth of the diameter
from the axis of the column.

The other processes of finding the shades and shadows
are sufficiently shown by the construction, and require no
further comment.

Figure 66 shows the shadows of the capital of a
detached column with lintel lines.

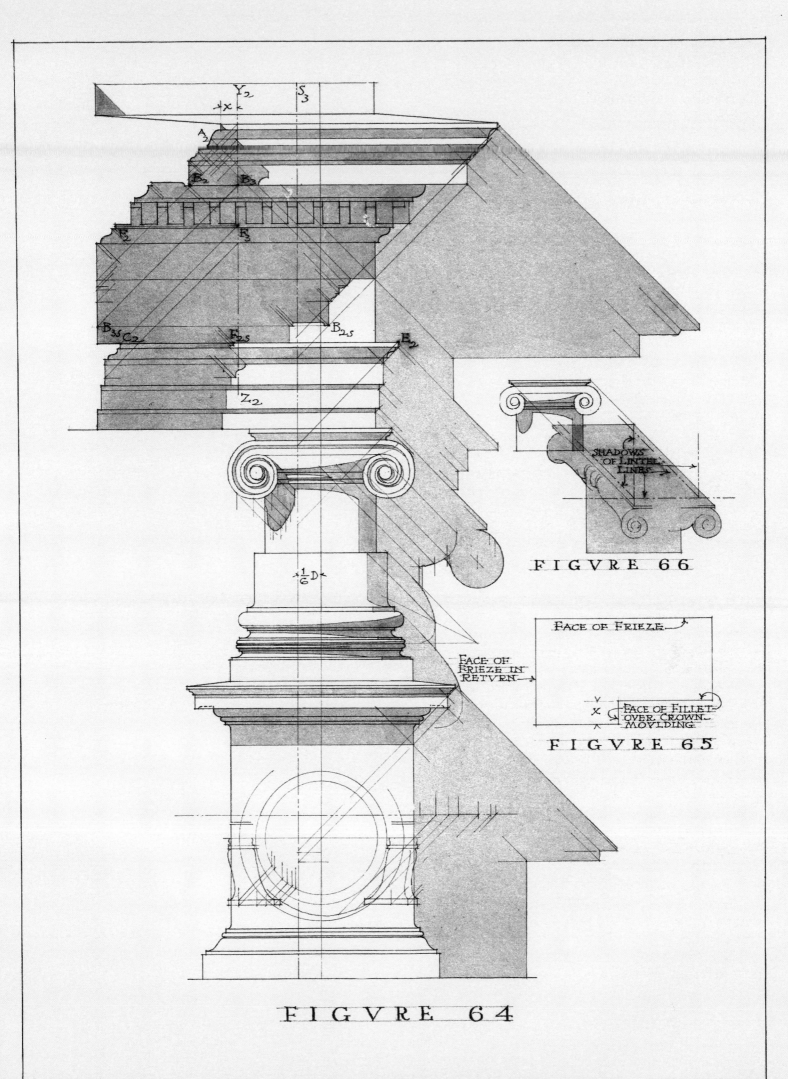

Y_2 S_3

x

A_2

B_2 B_3

F_2 F_3

B_{35} C_2 $F_{2.5}$ $B_{2.5}$ E_2

Z_2

$\frac{1}{6}$ D

SHADOWS
OF LINTEL
LINES

FIGVRE 66

FACE OF FRIEZE

FACE OF
FRIEZE IN
RETVRN

FACE OF FILLET
OVER CROWN
MOVLDING

FIGVRE 65

FIGVRE 64

The Shades and Shadows of the Angular Ionic Order according to Scamozzi

The order shown in Figure 67 is engaged one-third of the lower diameter of the column in a wall behind it. The shadow of the abacus is cast by direct projection, the plan being used. The shadows of the volutes are found by casting the shadows of the rectangles circumscribing the faces of the volutes, and then inscribing in these auxiliary shadows the oblique projections of the faces of the volutes. The part $A_{2S} B_{2S}$ of the shadow on the wall is the shadow of the ovolo of the capital.

The other parts of the shades and shadows require no comment.

Figure 68 shows the shadows of a detached column, etc., with lintel lines.

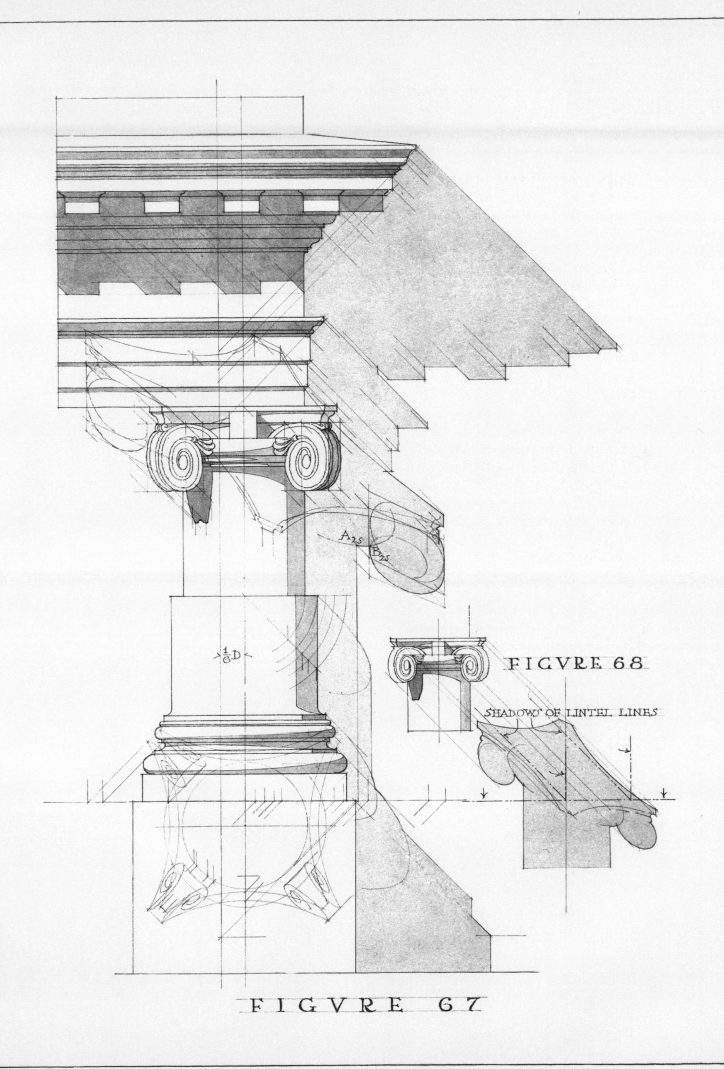

$\frac{1}{6}$ D

A₂₅
B₂₅

FIGVRE 68

SHADOWS OF LINTEL LINES

FIGVRE 67

The Shades and Shadows
of the Corinthian Order

Figure 69 shows the shades and shadows of the Corinthian order according to Vignola. The order is engaged one-third of the lower diameter of the column in a wall behind it.

The shadows on the entablature present no difficulty.

There is no practicable method for determining the whole of the shades and shadows on the capital. The shades on the tips of the leaves may be found by regarding those leaves as parts of tori, and other partial shadows, such as those on the abacus, may be determined geometrically according to methods previously given; but many of these shades and shadows must be drawn from imagination, or with the help of an actual model.

The shadow of the capital on the wall is subject to the same difficulties. It may be determined with reasonable certainty, however, by casting shadows of the abacus, those of rectangles containing approximately the volutes, those of circles containing tips of the leaves, and those of the ribs of those leaves which will evidently cast shadow. Around the shadows of the ribs of the leaves, the oblique projections of the leaves may be drawn from imagination, the process being similar to that of casting the shadows of the modillions as explained in Article XXVII. The shadow of the capital in Figure 69 was cast in this way.

In Figure 69 it is assumed that the entablature returns along the wall at the right of the column. In that case the shadows of modillions A and B fall on top of the taenia at A_{2s} and B_{2s} and are not visible in elevation. If the wall were unbroken the shadow would take the form shown by the dotted line.

Figure 70 shows the shadow, with dotted lintel lines, of an unengaged column.

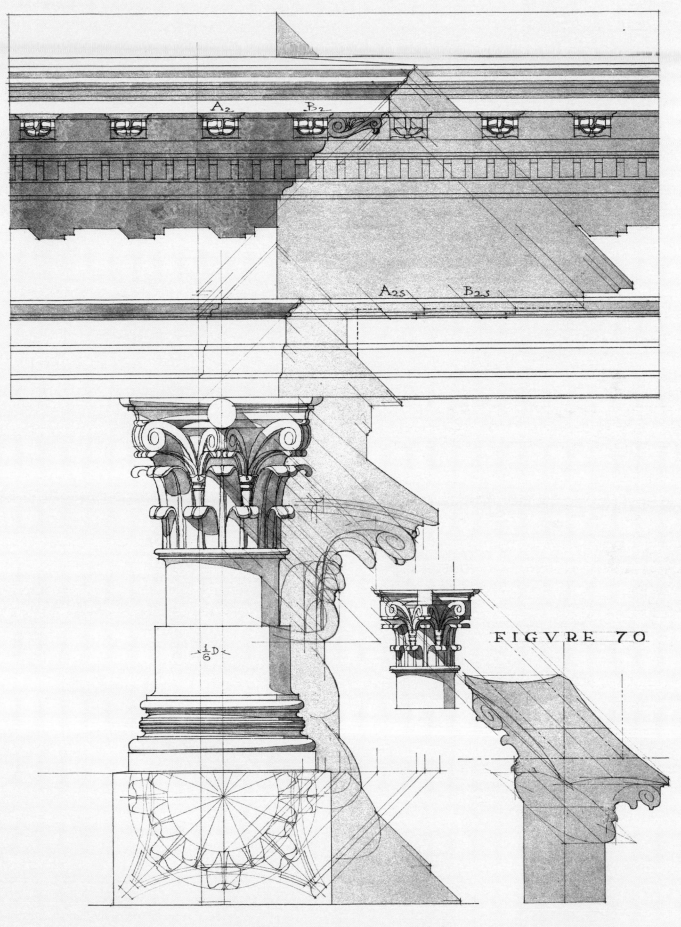

A₂ B₂

A₂₅ B₂₅

⅙D

FIGVRE 70

FIGVRE 69

The Shades and Shadows
of the Composite Capital

Figure 71 shows the shades and shadows of the composite
capital of Vignola, the shadow being cast on a wall behind
the column. The method here shown for casting the
shadows of the leaves is of necessity only approximate, and
is the same as that detailed in Article XXXV, for casting
the shadow of the Corinthian capital. Compare the shade
of the capitals shown in this and in the preceding figures
with the shadows of the models of these orders shown in
Figures 77, 78 and 79. It should be noted that the models
used in these cases are not quite like the capitals shown in
Figures 69, 70 and 71. This fact partially accounts for some
differences between the shadows in the two cases.

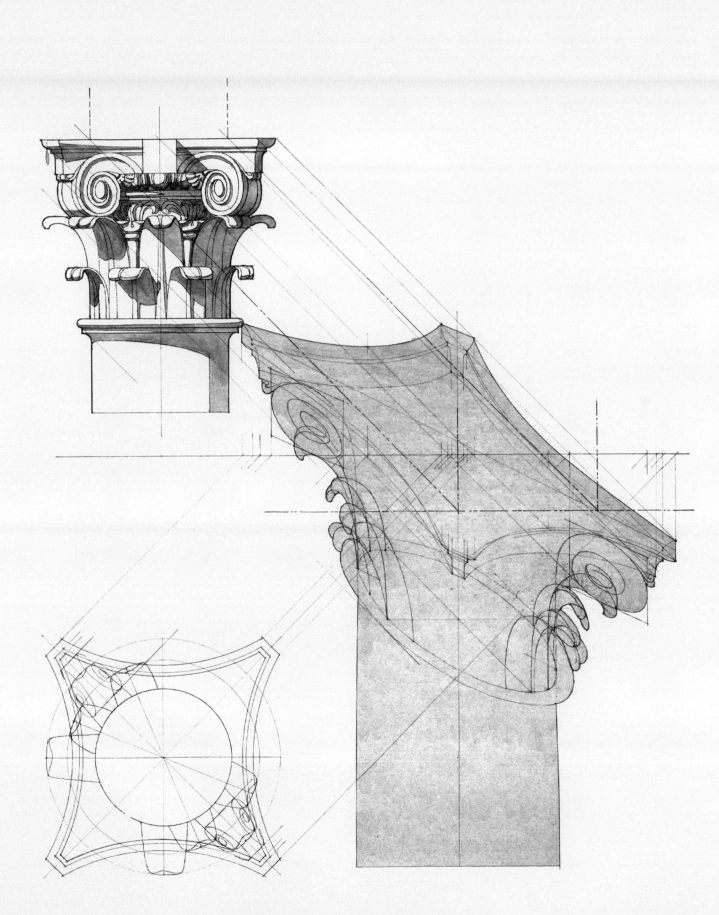

F I G V R E 71

FIGURES 72 TO 81.

Shades and Shadows
Photographed from Models

The following ten plates are made from photographs of models exposed to direct sunlight, having the conventional direction. The models were furnished for this purpose by Mr. Charles Emmel, Boston.

The method of obtaining the required direction of light was very simple, and was as follows: Upon a horizontal drawing-board, a sheet of paper was mounted. On the paper a square of convenient size was laid out. In these experiments, eight inches was made the side of the square. A diagonal of the square was drawn. With the corner of the square as a center and a radius equal to the diagonal, a circle was described. On this center was placed, perpendicular to the board, a sharp pointed rod, the length of which was eight inches, the length of the side of the square. Now, the rod representing one vertical edge of a cube, the square on the paper represented the bottom of that cube. When the shadow of the tip of the rod fell on the corner of the square diagonally opposite, the ray casting that shadow coincided with the diagonal of the cube, and hence the ray had the conventional direction.

It is evident that a line drawn from the tip of the rod to any point on the circle above described would make the same angle with the horizontal as did the ray from the tip to the opposite corner of the square. Hence, whenever the shadow of the tip of the rod fell on the circle at any point the sun had the conventional altitude; that is, the rays of light made the angle r with the horizontal plane.

The sun of course has the required altitude twice each day, once in the morning and again in the afternoon, at hours varying according to the time of the year and the latitude of the place. The accompanying photographs were made about half-past eight o'clock in the morning, in Philadelphia, in the latter part of August. At that time and place the sun had the same altitude near half-past three o'clock in the afternoon.

The direction r with reference to the vertical plane could evidently be obtained at any time by twisting that plane on a vertical axis until the shadow of a vertical line on a horizontal plane would make the angle forty-five degrees with the foot of the vertical plane. In these experiments the vertical plane was an upright screen before which the models were placed. This screen had a wide horizontal base to insure its steadiness. Upon this base was drawn a line making forty-five degrees with the foot of the screen. At a convenient point on this line a vertical rod eight inches high was placed. The screen was then twisted toward the light until the shadow of this vertical rod on the

horizontal base coincided with the forty-five-degree line through its foot, when the rays made the angle r with the screen. The rays were kept at this angle with the screen while photographs were being made by continually twisting the screen so as to keep the shadow of the rod on the forty-five-degree line.

The board with its upright rod above described being properly leveled, it was easy to tell when the rays were approaching the conventional direction with reference to the horizontal by watching the shadow of the tip of the rod approach the circle. When the shadow of the tip was on or very near the circle, the photographs were taken.

The rays having exactly the angle r only for an infinitesimally short time, no method of taking such photographs could give absolutely exact results. Several photographs were made at the time of each experiment, and the changing of models and of plates in the camera covered several minutes. The variation in the altitude of the sun during the time consumed in making any one lot of photographs was, however, not more than one degree; and as the angle r with the screen was kept correct by twisting the screen and its base on which the models stood, the variations of the shadows as photographed from those cast by rays having the angle absolutely correct would be almost imperceptible. At the time and place of making the photographs, the angle of the rays with the horizontal varied very nearly one degree in five minutes.

The photographs being made from a point at a finite distance from the objects, those objects show the perspective, not in true elevation. This would affect but slightly the pictures of the shadows on the screen, since they are in one plane; but it would affect the pictures of the models and of the shadows on them very considerably. To obviate this difficulty a telephoto lens was used and the camera placed as near as possible from the screen. Thus the effects of perspective were so far reduced as to be fairly negligible for models of the size and character used.

FIGURE 72.

The Shades and Shadows of the Ionic Order

Figure 72 shows the shades and shadows of the Ionic order of the Erechtheum at Athens. The column in not engaged, but is placed on axis, with an unmoulded pedestal under it. The diameter of the column shown is seven inches; and the pedestal is eleven inches square. The back of the pedestal was placed against the screen. Both pedestal and model were square with the screen.

The Shades and Shadows of the Ionic Order

FIGURE 73.

The Shades and Shadows of the Ionic Order

Figure 73 shows the shades and shadows of the same order
as the preceding figure, the pedestal being placed far enough
in front of the screen to show the whole of the shadows on
the screen of the capital and base.

The Shades and Shadows of the Ionic Order

FIGURE 74.

The Shades and Shadows of the Ionic Order

Figure 74 shows the shades and shadows of the same order as the preceding, the side of the capital being turned toward the front, as happens on the side of a portico which is more than one bay deep.

The Shades and Shadows of the Ionic Order

FIGURE 75.

The Shades and Shadows
of the Angular Ionic Order

Figure 75 shows the shades and shadows of the angular
Ionic order. The back of the pedestal was placed against
the screen, and the column on axis with the pedestal.

FIGURE 76.

The Shades and Shadows
of the Angular Ionic Order

Figure 76 shows the shades and shadows of the angular
Ionic order according to Scamozzi. The pedestal is placed
far enough in front of the screen to show the whole of
the shadows of the capital and base on the screen.

FIGURE 77.

The Shades and Shadows
of the Corinthian Order

Figure 77 shows the shades and shadows of the Corinthian
order, according to Vignola. The column is placed on axis
with the pedestal, and the back of the pedestal is set against
the screen.

FIGURE 78.

The Shades and Shadows
of the Corinthian Order

Figure 78 shows the shades and shadows of the Corinthian
order, according to Vignola. The column is placed on axis
with the pedestal, and the pedestal is set far enough in front
of the screen to show the whole of the shadows of the
capital and base on the screen.

FIGURE 79.

The Shades and Shadows
of the Composite Order

Figure 79 shows the shades and shadows of the Composite
order according to Vignola. The column is placed on axis
with the pedestal and the back of the pedestal is set against
the screen.

The Shades and Shadows
of the Composite Order

FIGURE 80.

The Shades and Shadows of the Ionic and Corinthian Pilaster Capitals

Figure 80 shows the shades and shadows of two pilaster capitals—the angular Ionic and the Corinthian. The capitals have a return on the side corresponding to a pilaster whose side is one-half its face.

FIGURE 81.

The Shades and Shadows
of a Modillion and of a Console

Figure 81 shows the shades and shadows of a Corinthian
modillion and of an Ionic console. Note that the tip
of the acanthus leaf of the modillion does not project
forward far enough to receive light and cast shadow, as is
the case with the modillions shown in Figures 51 and 69.

Index

Figure numbers are in italics